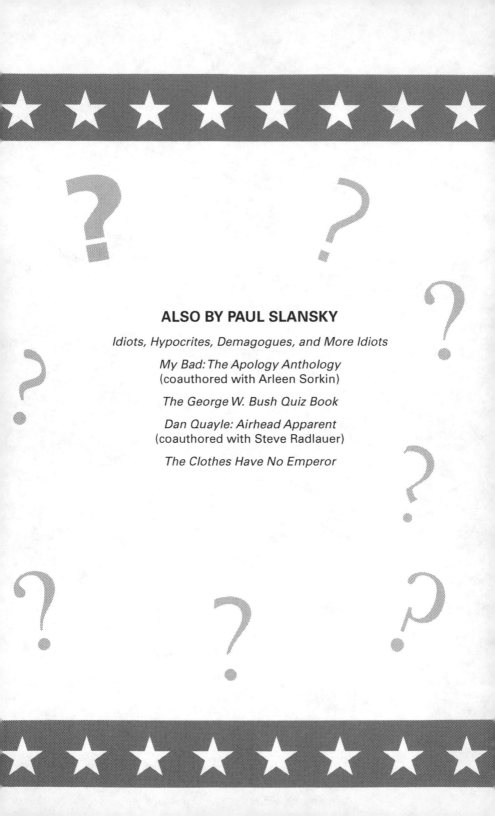

ALSO BY PAUL SLANSKY

Idiots, Hypocrites, Demagogues, and More Idiots

My Bad: The Apology Anthology
(coauthored with Arleen Sorkin)

The George W. Bush Quiz Book

Dan Quayle: Airhead Apparent
(coauthored with Steve Radlauer)

The Clothes Have No Emperor

THE
LITTLE QUIZ
BOOK OF
BIG POLITICAL
SEX
SCANDALS!

PAUL SLANSKY

SIMON & SCHUSTER PAPERBACKS

New York   London   Toronto   Sydney

Simon & Schuster Paperbacks
A Division of Simon & Schuster, Inc.
1230 Avenue of the Americas
New York, NY 10020

First Simon & Schuster trade paperback edition May 2009

SIMON & SCHUSTER PAPERBACKS and colophon are registered
trademarks of Simon & Schuster, Inc.

For information about special discounts for bulk purchases,
please contact Simon & Schuster Special Sales at
1-866-506-1949 or business@simonandschuster.com.

The Simon & Schuster Speakers Bureau can bring authors
to your live event. For more information or to book an event,
contact the Simon & Schuster Speakers Bureau at
1-866-248-3049 or visit our website at www.simonspeakers.com.

Designed by Jaime Putorti

Manufactured in the United States of America

10 9 8 7 6 5 4 3 2 1

Library of Congress Cataloging-in-Publication Data

Slansky, Paul.
The little quiz book of big political sex scandals / Paul Slansky.
    p. cm.
    1. Sex scandals—United States—History—Humor. 2. Politicians—Sexual
behavior—United States—History—Humor. 3. Presidents—Sexual behavior—
United States—History—Humor. 4. United States—Politics and government—
Humor. I. Title.
E183.S59 2009
302.2'4—dc22
                        2009001218

ISBN-13: 978-1-4165-9978-4
ISBN-10:   1-4165-9978-9

For Sarah Palin,
whose alleged affair with her secessionist hubby's business partner
*(http.//www.nationalenquirer.com/national_enquirer_world_*
exclusive_sarah_palins_secret_lover_revealed/celebrity/65481)
will surely receive further scrutiny if she continues to delude herself
into thinking she has a national political future

CONTENTS

THE
LITTLE QUIZ
BOOK OF
BIG POLITICAL
SEX
SCANDALS!

EIGHT PRESIDENTS

(PLUS ALEXANDER HAMILTON AND J. EDGAR HOOVER BECAUSE THERE WAS NO PLACE ELSE IN THE BOOK TO PUT THEM)

1. True or false? While living in the new nation's capital in Philadelphia, **ALEXANDER HAMILTON** had to endure not just being separated from his wife but also from his older sister.

    a. True. He enjoyed a particularly close relationship with her and missed her terribly.

    b. False. Hamilton had no sister. His wife, however, did, and in addition to being separated from his wife, he had to endure being separated from his wife's sister, with whom he'd been having an affair.

2. What did James Reynolds do in 1791 when he learned that his wife, Maria, was having an affair with Alexander Hamilton?

    a. He began an affair with his wife's paramour's wife.

    b. He demanded financial compensation and received more than $1,000 in exchange for not stopping the affair.

    c. He challenged the man who was cuckolding him to a duel, then chickened out and didn't show up.

3. How did James Reynolds learn of his wife's affair?

    a. His mother told him.

    b. He found the gentleman in question's scarf in her coat pocket.

    c. He walked in on her first assignation, suggesting to historians that the whole thing might have been a setup that he was in on.

4. How did James Reynolds make his living?

    a. Publishing.

    b. Banking.

    c. Swindling.

5. What did Alexander Hamilton do when James Reynolds claimed that Hamilton was paying him for inside tips about government securities?

    a. He challenged Reynolds to a duel, but Reynolds chickened out and didn't show up.

    b. He arranged for Reynolds to be arrested in connection with another matter entirely.

    c. He explained that he was actually paying Reynolds for the right to sleep with his wife, confessed the affair—an "indelicate amour," he called it—and made his love letters public as proof.

6. What was the great coincidence connected to the Hamilton-Reynolds affair?

    a. Maria Reynolds's lawyer in her subsequent divorce proceedings against James was Aaron Burr, who went on to kill Hamilton in a duel in 1804.

    b. When the man who bought Debbie Reynolds's Beverly Hills mansion in 1975 got married, his best man was George Hamilton.

    c. Musicians named Hamilton and Reynolds were two thirds of a rock band that had two top-five hits ("Don't Pull Your Love" and "Fallin' In Love") in the 1970s.

7. What family connection was **THOMAS JEFFERSON** said to have to Sally Hemings, the slave with whom he is alleged to have had anywhere from one to five children?

    a. She was his wife's half sister.

    b. She was his half sister.

    c. She was his sister-in-law's first cousin.

8. True or false? **JAMES BUCHANAN**'s lifelong bachelorhood included more than a dozen live-in relationships with women.

    a. True. In addition to those he lived with, he was believed to have slept with close to a thousand women, which could put him ahead of John Kennedy and even Bill Clinton in this particular sweepstakes.

    b. False. It included a fifteen-year live-in relationship with Alabama senator William Rufus de Vane King, whom people referred to as "his wife," as well as "Miss Nancy" and "Aunt Fancy." In addition to being known as possibly our first gay president, his having overseen the secession of seven states from the Union and having led the nation to the brink of the Civil War make him the only chief executive who could conceivably give George W. Bush a run for the title of Worst President Ever.

9. What historical distinction does **JAMES GARFIELD** hold?

    a. He's the only member of the House of Representatives elected directly to the presidency.

    b. His six-month 1881 tenure as president is the second shortest, while the two months spent slowly dying after being shot four months after taking office far and away holds the record for lingering.

    c. Both of the above, plus he's the first president known to have had an extramarital affair, though it was years before his brief stay in the White House.

10. False or true? **GROVER CLEVELAND** was elected president in 1884 despite having been widely believed to have fathered an illegitimate child.

    a. False. He was defeated by James G. Blaine.

    b. True. Even he wasn't sure about the child's paternity, because apparently the lady in question, Maria Crofts Halpin, had had several, ahem, suitors, but after having been the butt of his opponent's mocking campaign "Ma, Ma, where's my pa?", he and his supporters had the last-laugh response, "Gone to the White House, ha, ha, ha!"

11. True or false? Though his presidency instantly devolved into a scandal-ridden fiasco, **WARREN G. HARDING** was telling the truth when he assured Republican party bosses who were inclined to nominate him for the presidency in 1920 that his life up to that point was unblemished by impropriety.

    a. True. It was only upon taking office that Harding's baser instincts were given free rein.

    b. False. He was lying through his teeth, given that he had not one but two mistresses at the time, not to mention an illegitimate child.

12. True or false? To keep news of then presidential candidate Warren Harding's affair with Carrie Fulton Phillips, the wife of a friend of his, from coming out during the campaign, the Republican National Committee paid the woman at least $50,000 in hush money.

    a. False. The suggestion was made by the committee chairman, but Harding vetoed the option because of its "troubling immorality."

    b. True. They also sent her and her family to Japan for the duration of the campaign, and made monthly payments to her following his election.

13. According to her book *The President's Daughter*, Nan Britton conceived an illegitimate daughter with Warren Harding in his Senate office. Where did she say they had sex after he became president?

    a. In a coat closet next to the Oval Office.

    b. In a bathroom off of the Oval Office.

    c. On Harding's Oval Office desk.

14. How did **FRANKLIN D. ROOSEVELT** meet his mistress Lucy Mercer?

    a. She was a reporter for the *Harvard Crimson* when he was the university's president.

    b. She was the social secretary of his wife, Eleanor.

    c. She was an administrator at the Warm Springs rehabilitation facility where he underwent hydrotherapy in a failed effort to overcome his paralysis.

15. Marguerite Alice (Missy) LeHand was Franklin Roosevelt's live-in lover at the White House. What was the name of Eleanor Roosevelt's live-in lover?

    a. Louella Adcock.

    b. Lorena Hickok.

    c. Loretta Hitchcock.

16. True or false? Hours before his death, Franklin Roosevelt asked to see Lucy Mercer, but by the time she arrived, he had died.

    a. True. She blamed her assistant, who had initially forgotten to give her the message, and would have fired her but for the fact that the assistant felt so guilty and was so distraught that she accidentally walked in front of a bus and was killed.

    b. False. She was with him at his estate in Warm Springs, Georgia, on the day he died, though not at his bedside when he took his last breath.

17. True or false? The first hint that the public had that **DWIGHT EISENHOWER** had been unfaithful to his wife, Mamie, came in Kay Summersby's 1975 deathbed memoir, *Past Forgetting: My Love Affair with Dwight D. Eisenhower.*

   a. True. Mamie claimed to have known all about it.

   b. False. The affair was first mentioned two years earlier, in *Plain Speaking: An Oral Biography of Harry S Truman*, in which author Merle Miller quotes Truman as saying, "Why, right after the war was over [Eisenhower] wrote a letter to General Marshall saying that he wanted to be relieved of duty, saying that he wanted to come back to the United States and divorce Mrs. Eisenhower so that he could marry this English-woman." And Mamie never said anything publicly about any of it.

18. What did Kay Summersby reveal about Dwight Eisenhower's sexual appetites?

   a. He was insatiable, and thrice-daily encounters were not uncommon.

   b. Threesomes were his favorite.

   c. He was impotent and they never consummated their affair.

19. What did **LYNDON B. JOHNSON**'s mistress Madeleine Duncan Brown say that the then vice president told her the night before the assassination of President Kennedy that, in retrospect, seemed to imply his possible involvement in that event?

   a. "I hope Jackie looks good in black."

   b. "After tomorrow those SOBs will never embarrass me again."

   c. "Wake me if a fella named Lee calls."

20. What else did Lyndon Johnson's mistress say about the Kennedy assassination?

  a. She'd seen Lee Harvey Oswald with Jack Ruby in the latter's strip joint.

  b. A month after the assassination, Johnson told her it had been a CIA/Texas oil industry plot.

  c. Both of the above, plus after it was decided in 1960 that Kennedy would be the presidential nominee and Johnson would be his running mate, oil tycoon and Johnson supporter H. L. Hunt "made the remark, 'We may have lost a battle but we're going to win a war,' and then the day of the assassination he said, 'Well, we won the war.'"

21. What led to the 1964 resignation of Lyndon Johnson's aide **WALTER JENKINS**?

  a. He was forced once too often to lie to Lady Bird Johnson about her husband's extramarital activities.

  b. He was arrested in the same Washington, D.C., YMCA men's room that he'd been arrested in five years earlier for similar "disorderly conduct."

  c. He became convinced that his boss was involved in the Kennedy assassination.

22. According to Anthony Summers's gossipy biography, what was **J. EDGAR HOOVER**, the FBI chief from 1935 until his death in 1972, said to do periodically?

  a. Camp out all night in the bushes outside the home of someone he despised, hoping to "see something."

  b. Get drunk and obsess about how to retrieve the photos the Mafia was said to have of him and his associate FBI director Clyde Tolson—two lifelong bachelors who worked together, ate together, went to nightclubs together, vacationed together, and are buried side by side—having sex.

c. Cross-dress, including one sighting—by a source, it should be noted, with a serious beef against the FBI—in which "He was wearing a fluffy black dress, very fluffy, with flounces, and lace stockings and high heels, and a black curly wig. He had makeup on, and false eyelashes. It was a very short skirt, and he was sitting there in the living room of the suite with his legs crossed. Roy [Cohn] introduced him to me as 'Mary' and he replied, 'Good evening,' brusque, like the first time I'd met him. It was obvious he wasn't a woman, you could see where he shaved. It was Hoover. You've never seen anything like it. I couldn't believe it that I should see the head of the FBI dressed up as a woman."

23. What was Richard Nixon reported to have said upon hearing of the death of J. Edgar Hoover?
  a. "Jesus Christ! That old cocksucker!"
  b. "Rose Mary, be sure to send a condolence card to the widow Tolson."
  c. "Hah! I wonder who's gonna get the red dress and the black feather boa. You know who it'd look good on? That pansy Roy Cohn."

24. What nickname accrued to J. Edgar Hoover as a result of all the rumors?
  a. J. Edna Hoover.
  b. Jaye Edgar Hoover.
  c. Both of the above, plus "Gay Edgar Hoover."

25. GEORGE H. W. BUSH, aka "Poppy" and married to an unpleasant woman who looked more like his mother than his wife, was credibly rumored to have had an affair at some point with his longtime executive assistant—an affair that was neither admitted nor proven, and about which, when asked by NBC's Stone Phillips, he said, "You're perpetuating the sleaze by even asking the question, to say nothing of asking it in the Oval Office," and about which rumored adultery his dim-witted ne'er-do-well eldest son told a magazine, "The answer to the Big A question is N.O." What was the name of the assistant?

 a. Jennifer Fitzpatrick.
 b. Jennifer Fitzgerald.
 c. Jennifer Fitzsimmons.

★ ★ ★ ★ ★

ANSWERS: 1. *b*, 2. *b*, 3. *c*, 4. *c*, 5. *c*, 6. *a*, 7. *a*, 8. *b*, 9. *c*, 10. *b*, 11. *b*, 12. *b*, 13. *a*, 14. *b*, 15. *b*, 16. *b*, 17. *b*, 18. *c*, 19. *b*, 20. *c*, 21. *b*, 22. *c*, 23. *a*, 24. *c*, 25. *b*.

THANKS, POPPY!

In the great tradition of doofus White House sibs such as Roger Clinton and Billy Carter came **NEIL BUSH,** *the third of four sons-of-Bushes and, as bad as he is, only the second worst.*

1. In which countries did Neil Bush, traveling on business to Asia in the late 1990s, occasionally open his hotel room door to find women he'd never met offering themselves to him— offers that he invariably took them up on?

- **a.** Hong Kong and Thailand.
- **b.** Indonesia and Cambodia.
- **c.** India and Nepal.
- **d.** Vietnam and China.

2. What company was Neil Bush representing on those Asian trips that might have had something to do with paying those women to show up at the well-connected son of a former president's hotel room door?

- **a.** Grace Semiconductor.
- **b.** Transmedia.
- **c.** Apex Energy.
- **d.** Arbusto Oil.

3. How did Neil Bush inform Sharon, his wife of twenty-three years and the mother of his three children, that he was leaving her for another woman?

- **a.** He took her out to an expensive dinner and broke the news over a bottle of wine.
- **b.** His cell phone accidentally dialed hers and she heard him talking to a friend about it.
- **c.** He sent her an e-mail.

4. How did Neil Bush respond when his wife's divorce lawyer said, "Mr. Bush, you have to admit that it's a pretty remarkable thing for a man just to go to a hotel room door and open it and have a woman standing there and have sex with her"?

    a. "It was very unusual."

    b. "I don't have to admit anything. That's the beauty of being a Bush."

    c. "You get used to it."

5. True or false? Neil Bush's ex-wife, Sharon, said she took hair samples from Neil's head to use in a voodoo doll she was making.

    a. True. She had help from a Haitian housekeeper.

    b. False. While many people believe the voodoo story, she said she took Neil's hairs so they could be tested for drugs.

6. Fill in the blank: Neil Bush was on the board of _____ Savings and Loan when it collapsed in 1988 (costing taxpayers well over $1 billion), and though no criminal charges were filed, an expert hired by federal regulators found that he had "an ethical disability" that allowed him to engage in "the worst kinds of conflict of interest."

    a. Lincoln

    b. Silverado

    c. Home State

7. True or false? Neil Bush was contrite after the savings and loan collapse his actions helped to bring about.

    a. True. He realized he'd brought shame on the family.

    b. False. He was belligerent in the face of having been found morally lacking, insisting patronizingly, despite all evidence to the contrary, "There. Was. No. Conflict. Of. Interest." (Read his lips!) As writer Steven Wilmsen observed in *Playboy*, "He seemed to believe it was his birthright to profit at the nation's expense."

8. Complete historian Kevin Phillips's assessment of Neil Bush's career: "He's incorrigible. He seems to be crawling through the _____ of crony capitalism."

   a. gutters

   b. sewers

   c. underbelly

When President Bush nominated **CLARENCE THOMAS** *to the Supreme Court in 1991, he claimed it was not for the sublime cynicism of getting a hard right-winger to fill the black seat previously held by ultraliberal Thurgood Marshall, but rather because he was "the best man for the job on the merits." Said it with a straight face, too, yes he did.*

9. Three of these quotes come from Anita Hill's testimony at the Clarence Thomas confirmation hearings. Which one was offered as confirmation of his bad behavior by another harassed former Thomas employee?

   a. "After a brief discussion of work, he would turn the conversation to a discussion of sexual matters. His conversations were very vivid. He spoke about acts that he had seen in pornographic films involving such matters as women having sex with animals and films showing group sex or rape scenes."

   b. "He talked about pornographic materials depicting individuals with large penises or large breasts involving various sex acts. On several occasions, Thomas told me graphically of his own sexual prowess."

   c. "I just felt like he got a certain amount of pleasure out of saying certain things to women."

   d. "He referred to the size of his own penis as being larger than normal, and he also spoke on some occasions of the pleasures he had given to women with oral sex."

10. Who was that other harassed former Clarence Thomas underling who supported Anita Hill's story—by telling Senate investigators that Thomas nagged her to date him (saying things like "You will be going out with me" or "When I get around to dating you"), inquired about details of her anatomy ("What size are your breasts?"), and showed up at her apartment decidedly uninvited—and yet somehow was never brought before the public to testify at the hearings?
  a. Andrea Wright.
  b. Angela Wright.
  c. Anthea Wright.

11. False or true? When it was Clarence Thomas's turn to defend himself against the charges made by Anita Hill, he claimed not to have listened to her testimony.
  a. False. He wanted to say it, just to show her how little he thought of her, how unimportant she was to him, but he knew no one would believe him.
  b. True. He insisted repeatedly that he'd refused to listen to all those "lies," and no one called him on the absurdity of his claim.

12. What porn character did Clarence Thomas mention appreciatively to Anita Hill?
  a. Johnny Wadd.
  b. Harry Reems.
  c. Long Dong Silver.

13. Complete Clarence Thomas's unusual question to Anita Hill: "Who has put pubic hair on my _____?"
  a. Coke
  b. cock
  c. toothbrush

14. In his effort to suggest that Anita Hill got her story about Clarence Thomas's inquiry about the placement of pubic hair from a book, what novel did Senator Orrin Hatch (R-UT) wave around and read a passage from in which a character referred to "an alien pubic hair floating around in my gin"?

   a. *The Bonfire of the Vanities.*
   b. *The Exorcist.*
   c. *Hollywood Wives.*

15. Two of the following paragraphs refer to ABC News's Peter Jennings. Which one describes CBS's Dan Rather?

   a. When the Clarence Thomas hearings carried over into the weekend, he appeared on his network on Saturday morning to explain to disappointed kids why they weren't going to get their cartoons, saying, "We have been watching a woman, who's a lawyer, and a man, who's a judge, have a very painful disagreement about something the woman says the man did to her when they were working together. Though he never touched her, she says he said many things to her which were mean and disgusting, which made her feel threatened and really bad."

   b. At one point he got so caught up in the proceedings that he wondered, "Who and where happens next?"

   c. When Orrin Hatch said that Anita Hill was "caught up in a very clever embroilment," and added, "I don't want to call her a liar," he replied, "You already have, Senator."

16. Four of these statements describe Senator Orrin Hatch. Which four describe Senator Alan Simpson (R-WY)?

    a. He got so pissed off at his friend Ted Kennedy's pro–Anita Hill attitude that he blurted Freudian-slippingly at one point, "If you believe that, I've got a bridge in Massachusetts that I'll sell you."

    b. He referred to the remarks Anita Hill attributed to Clarence Thomas as "this foul, foul stack of stench" and a "garbage stench of verbiage," though it was clear that his outrage was not at him for saying them, but at her for making them up.

    c. He said to Clarence Thomas about Anita Hill's accusations, "The person who would do something like that . . . it seems to me, would not be a normal person. That person, it seems to me, would be a psychopathic sex fiend or a pervert." And where do we find such "perverted" people? "Generally, they're in insane asylums."

    d. He observed that the Senate had been dealing with the Clarence Thomas nomination for 105 days and that "We've seen everything, known everything, heard every bit of dirt, as you call it so well. And what do we know about Professor Hill? Not very much. I'm waiting for 105 days of surveillance of Ms. Hill, and then we'll see, you know, who ate the cabbage, as we say out in the Wild West."

    e. He claimed to be "getting stuff over the transom," receiving phone calls and letters about Anita Hill warning, "Watch out for this woman!" though he was unable to back up this ominous McCarthyism with any, you know, proof.

    f. He said of Anita Hill's testimony, "I don't know where she gets these things."

g. He said of Anita Hill's testimony, "Anyone can bring up issues of penises and breasts and that kind of thing."

h. In the course of questioning Clarence Thomas, he managed to utter the phrase "Long Dong Silver" more than half a dozen times: "Did you ever use the term 'Long Dong Silver'? . . . How could this quiet, retiring woman know about something like 'Long Dong Silver'? . . . Is that a black stereotype, something like 'Long Dong Silver'? . . . A picture of 'Long Dong Silver,' a photo of a black male with an elongated penis . . . the reference to 'Long Dong Silver,' which I find totally offensive . . . You never did talk to her about 'Long Dong Silver' . . . These two FBI agents told her to be as specific as she could possibly be, and yet she never said anything about 'Long Dong Silver.'"

17. Clarence Thomas was confirmed by the Senate with the smallest majority in history. What was the vote?

   a. 51–49.
   b. 52–48.
   c. 54–46.

18. According to his bitter memoir *My Grandfather's Son*, Clarence Thomas was in the bathtub when his wife came in to tell him his Supreme Court nomination had been confirmed. What was his scornful response?

   a. "Zip-a-dee-doo-dah!"
   b. "Whoop-de-damn-doo!"
   c. "Yabba-dabba-doo!"

19. "By the time he reached Yale law school . . . Thomas was known not only for the extreme crudity of his sexual banter, but also for avidly watching pornographic films and reading pornographic magazines, which he would describe to his friends in lurid detail. . . . Colleagues recall that Thomas was notable for the unusually public nature of his enthusiasm for pornographic details—his detailed descriptions of the movies, the magazines he had seen were an open form of socializing during these years. . . . It is for this reason that when Anita Hill accused Thomas of talking to her crudely about sexual matters, which she found strange, a number of otherwise impartial schoolmates of Thomas' were struck by the familiarity of the behavior." What was the name of the book by Jane Mayer and Jill Abramson that reported the above?

    a. *Strange Justice: The Selling of Clarence Thomas.*
    b. *High Tech Lynching: The Self-Pity of Clarence Thomas.*
    c. *His Grandfather's Son.*

20. After speaking a total of 281 words during the 2004–2005 and 2005–2006 terms of the Supreme Court, what did Clarence Thomas do during the 2006–2007 term?

    a. He suddenly became the most garrulous of all the justices.
    b. He said the same 281 words, only this time in a single term.
    c. He uttered not a single syllable.

21. Which rapper said, "The white man ain't the devil, I promise/ You want to see the devil, take a look at Clarence Thomas"?

    a. KRS-One.
    b. Kanye West.
    c. Jay-Z.

22. Which aspect of Clarence Thomas's personality has been most frequently commented on over the years?

a. His open-mindedness.

b. His honesty.

c. His howling rage.

ANSWERS: 1. *a*, 2. *a*, 3. *c*, 4. *a*, 5. *b*, 6. *b*, 7. *b*, 8. *c*, 9. *c*, 10. *b*, 11. *b*, 12. *c*, 13. *a*, 14. *b*, 15. *b*, 16. Hatch: *a, c, f, h*, Simpson: *b, d, e, g*, 17. *b*, 18. *b*, 19. *a*, 20. *c*, 21. *a*, 22. *c*.

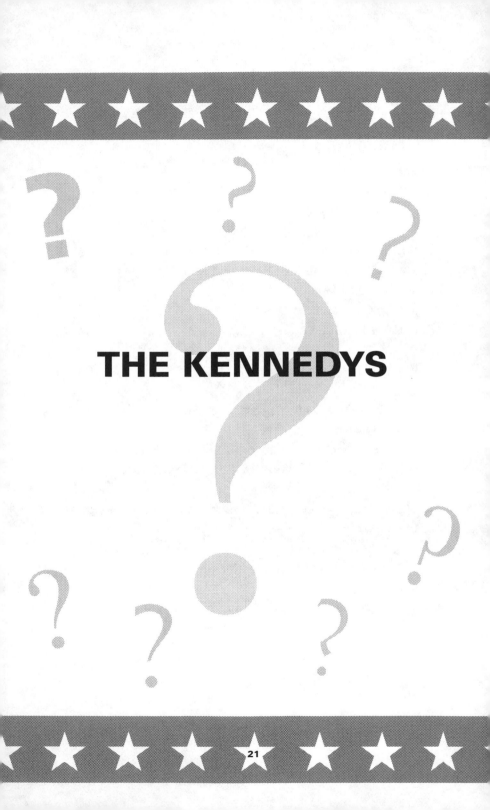

THE KENNEDYS

1. Who introduced Judith Campbell Exner – then merely Judith Campbell—to Senator and future president **JOHN F. KENNEDY** in Las Vegas in early 1960?
- **a.** Peter Lawford.
- **b.** Dean Martin.
- **c.** Frank Sinatra.

2. Which Mafia boss was Judith Campbell involved with while she was also sleeping with President Kennedy?
- **a.** Paul Castellano.
- **b.** Sam Giancana.
- **c.** Carlo Gambino.

3. What did the two men have in common, besides Ms. Campbell, in 1961?
- **a.** Both of them were huge fans of the TV series *The Untouchables*.
- **b.** Both of them suffered from Addison's Disease.
- **c.** Both of them had assassination in their futures.

4. What were the Secret Service nicknames for the blonde and brunette White House secretaries President Kennedy was sleeping with?
- **a.** Tweedle Dumb and Tweedle Dumber.
- **b.** Fiddle and Faddle.
- **c.** Twiddle and Twaddle.

Who is reported to have said what about President Kennedy?

5. Marilyn Monroe.

    a. "[It was] the most remarkable sixty seconds of my life."

6. Judith Campbell Exner.

    b. "I used to say that the Kennedy men were morally bankrupt. And I still feel that way."

7. Angie Dickinson.

    c. "Well, let's put it this way. I've had better. He's a little too quick to suit me. But he seems to be a fast learner."

8. Two of these JFK mistresses met violent deaths within four years of his assassination. Which one predeceased him?

    a. Mary Pinchot Meyer.

    b. Marilyn Monroe.

    c. Jayne Mansfield.

9. False or true? A *Newsweek* reporter covering **TED KENNEDY** in the spring of 1969 warned his editor that the Massachusetts senator was "under terrible stress, an accident waiting to happen," and a *Life* reporter told her editors, "He's living by his gut; something bad is going to happen."

    a. False. To the press, Kennedy always seemed completely in control.

    b. True. The murder of the second of one's two older brothers would test the mettle of someone of the strongest character, so it's only logical that it would devastate someone as flawed as he.

10. What were some of the early-in-life clues that Ted Kennedy might not react honorably or calmly in the event of an emergency?

    a. Faced with the possibility that a failing grade might keep him off the varsity football team, he hired someone to take a Spanish exam for him and was expelled from Harvard.

    b. He got into three fistfights with members of the opposing team in a single college rugby match, becoming the only player the referee kicked out of a game in his thirty-year career.

    c. Both of the above, plus once when several men on a nearby yacht shouted things at him that he didn't like, he boarded their boat and threw eight of them into the water, though he had no idea who could swim.

11. Why had the young women who had worked on Bobby Kennedy's tragic campaign—among them, Mary Jo Kopechne—chosen the third weekend of July in 1969 for their Martha's Vineyard reunion?

    a. It was the only time they were all available.

    b. That was when Ted Kennedy was competing in the Edgartown Yacht Club Regatta.

    c. They wanted to watch the moon landing together.

12. The reunion was held in a house on Chappaquiddick Island. Where were the motels at which the guests were staying?

    a. Chilmark.

    b. West Tisbury.

    c. Edgartown.

13. What time was it when Ted Kennedy said he wanted to go back to his room, and Mary Jo Kopechne said she wanted to leave, too, and could he give her a lift?
  a. About 10:15 P.M.
  b. About 11:15 P.M.
  c. About 12:15 A.M.

14. What made the judge conclude that "Kennedy and Kopechne did not intend to return to Edgartown at that time, that Kennedy did not intend to drive to the ferry slip, and his turn onto Dike Road was intentional"?
  a. Kopechne had not told any of the five other women at the party that she was going back to the hotel.
  b. Kopechne left her pocketbook at the party house.
  c. Both of the above, plus Kennedy was usually driven by his chauffeur but for some reason this time he asked for the keys to drive himself.

Match the number with what it quantifies.

15. Seventeen. **a.** Hours that passed between the time that Ted Kennedy drove his car off Dike Bridge with Mary Jo Kopechne inside it and his reporting of the accident to the police.
16. Eight. **b.** Phone calls made by Ted Kennedy before he placed one to the police.
17. Forty. **c.** Number of years Dike Bridge existed before someone managed to drive off of it.

18. Arrange these women in the order they were called by Ted Kennedy and informed of the accident.
  a. His wife, Joan.
  b. Mary Jo Kopechne's mother, Gwen.
  c. His longtime girlfriend Helga Wagner.
  d. His mother, Rose.

19. What did Ted Kennedy say in his nationally televised speech a week after the accident?

   a. "Only reasons of health"—her pregnancy—kept his wife, Joan, from being with him at Chappaquiddick.

   b. There was "no truth whatever to the widely circulated suspicions of immoral conduct" on the part of him or Mary Jo Kopechne.

   c. He "was not driving under the influence of liquor."

   d. His post-accident behavior "made no sense to me at all."

   e. All of the above, plus he wondered "whether some awful curse actually did hang over all the Kennedys."

20. What was part of Ted Kennedy's inquest testimony six months after the accident?

   a. He was driving "approximately twenty miles an hour," definitely fast for someone on an unfamiliar dirt road on a small island, but then he took "no particular notice" of the fact that the road had stopped being paved.

   b. He didn't want his friends to tell the other girls about the accident because "I felt strongly that if these girls were notified that an accident had taken place and Mary Jo had, in fact, drowned, that it would only be a matter of seconds before all of those girls, who were long and dear friends of Mary Jo's, would go to the scene of the accident and enter the water with, I felt, a good chance that some serious mishap might have occurred to any one of them."

   c. Both of the above, plus in his hotel room he had maintained "hope all night long that, by some miracle, Mary Jo would have escaped from the car," and he told his friends that he didn't report the accident because he just felt like "somehow when they arrived in the morning that they were going to say that Mary Jo was still alive."

Who's who in connection with Chappaquiddick?

21. Joe Gargan.

a. The first reporter on the scene, who had questions that somehow hadn't occurred to the police, like how exactly did Ted Kennedy mistake a turnoff onto a dirt road for the continuation of the main paved road back to the ferry, and why did Kennedy walk the mile-plus back to the party house to get his friends to help rescue Kopechne instead of stopping at one of the houses he passed along the way and getting help there?

22. Tony Bettencourt.

b. Ted Kennedy's cousin, who helped try to rescue Mary Jo Kopechne and, when those efforts failed, went back to the party and didn't mention the accident to anyone.

23. Paul Markham.

c. Ted Kennedy's cousin's friend, a former U.S. attorney from Massachusetts, who helped try to rescue Mary Jo Kopechne and, when those efforts failed, went back to the party with Ted Kennedy's cousin and didn't mention the accident to anyone.

24. Russell G. Peachy.

d. The Shiretown Inn manager to whom Ted Kennedy complained about the noise from a nearby party, half an hour after getting back to his hotel after swimming an eighth of a mile back to the mainland from the island where he'd left a dead girl in his sunken car. And what was so urgent about getting back to that hotel anyway?

25. Christopher Look. **e.** The Chappaquiddick Island resident who asked Ted Kennedy, "Senator, do you know there's a girl found dead in your car?"

26. John Farrar. **f.** The diver who found Mary Jo Kopechne's body and opined that she had located an air pocket and lived for two hours before it was used up, and that he could have had her out of the car alive in twenty-five minutes if only he'd been called.

27. Dominick J. Arena. **g.** The deputy sheriff who testified that between 12:30 and 12:45 A.M. that night (more than an hour later than Ted Kennedy claimed to have driven off the bridge) he saw a car with a man driving and a woman in the front seat—and how many of those do you think there were out there at that hour on this minimally populated island, let alone out there in a car with a license plate that matched at least one L and two 7s with Kennedy's Oldsmobile—and they seemed to be lost so he called out to help them and the car took off down Dike Road, almost as if, one might think, they'd been doing something they didn't want anyone to know about. So maybe Ted Kennedy didn't splash around in the water seven or eight times trying to save Mary Jo Kopechne. Maybe that time passed with the two of them having sex, and then they were heading back to the house when a stranger spotted them and Kennedy panicked and drove onto the dirt road to avoid being seen with the woman, and then he drove into the water while trying to make a U-turn to get back to the main road. Maybe.

28. Ed Joyce.

h. The Edgartown police chief who swallowed Ted Kennedy's story whole, until a CBS reporter showed up and pointed out the rather obvious holes in it.

29. James A. Boyle.

i. The judge who gave Ted Kennedy a two-month suspended sentence for leaving the scene of the accident, then later concluded that he hadn't told the truth but still chose not to have him arrested.

30. True or false? The judge was justified in citing Ted Kennedy's "unblemished record" as a reason for suspending his minimal two-month sentence.

a. True. Kennedy's clean driving record was one of the reasons the accident was so surprising.

b. False. The unblemishedness of his record was compromised by four reckless-driving citations for things such as running red lights and roaring through suburban streets at ninety miles per hour with his lights off.

31. Despite his persistent efforts, which of these women was Ted Kennedy never linked with romantically?
- **a.** Actress Candice Bergen.
- **b.** Socialite Amanda Burden.
- **c.** Skier Suzy Chaffee.
- **d.** Socialite Lacey Neuhaus.
- **e.** Oil heiress Page Lee Hufty.

32. Where was Ted Kennedy photographed in 1982 strolling fat and naked on a public beach?
- **a.** Palm Beach.
- **b.** Malibu.
- **c.** Cannes.

33. True or false? During the 1980s, Ted Kennedy developed a serious marijuana problem.
- **a.** True. According to an anonymous staff member, he put on more than a hundred pounds because of the munchies.
- **b.** False. He reportedly became a total cokehead, to the point where he'd show up at his Senate office with white powder on his nose.

34. What senator, seeing a *National Enquirer* photo of Ted Kennedy on top of some woman on a boat in the Mediterranean, said, "Well, I see Kennedy has changed his position on offshore drilling"?
- **a.** Howell Heflin.
- **b.** Orrin Hatch.
- **c.** Bob Dole.

35. In December 1985, at what D.C. restaurant did Ted Kennedy toss a waitress onto his seated friend Senator Chris Dodd (D-CT) and then proceed to jump on top and rub his crotch against the sandwiched woman?

    a. Duke Zeibert's.

    b. La Colline.

    c. La Brasserie.

36. In September 1987, at what D.C. restaurant was Ted Kennedy dining in a private room when a waitress walked in and found him on the floor on top of a young blonde lobbyist?

    a. La Brasserie.

    b. The Palm.

    c. Morton's.

37. False or true? Ted Kennedy was with his son Patrick and his nephew **WILLIAM KENNEDY SMITH** in a Palm Beach bar on Good Friday 1991 when Willie met the girl who would the next day accuse him of having raped her that night.

    a. False. Willie had invited him along but he decided to stay home and sleep.

    b. True, and the funny thing about that is that both men had been home, safely asleep, when Ted woke them up to go and "have a few beers" with him.

Who's who?

38. Patricia Bowman.

a. Went home with William Kennedy Smith, went for a walk on the beach with him, and, she said, got raped (though the jury acquitted him).

39. Audra Soulias.

b. Went home with William Kennedy Smith's cousin Patrick.

40. Michelle Cassone.

c. Brought a civil action against her former boss William Kennedy Smith in 2004 for raping her in 1999 (though the lawsuit was dismissed).

41. Which tabloid's publication of the name of the alleged rape victim was cited by the *New York Times* and NBC News as justification for them to publish it as well?

  a. *National Enquirer.*
  b. *Star.*
  c. *Globe.*

Match the number with what it quantifies.

42. Three.

a. Number of women whose stories of also having been sexually assaulted by William Kennedy Smith were deemed inadmissible by the judge.

43. Seventy-seven.

b. Minutes the jury deliberated before acquitting William Kennedy Smith.

44. True or false? In the wake of his involvement in the William Kennedy Smith incident—the image problems from which contributed mightily to his failure to enthusiastically fight the Clarence Thomas nomination—Ted Kennedy finally issued the full-on public apology for his behavior that his whole life had been leading up to.

    a. True. The speech, which included statements of remorse for eighteen individual incidents, lasted just over an hour.

    b. False. The closest he came was this sorta mea culpa in a 1991 speech in Boston: "I recognize my shortcomings—the faults in the conduct of my private life. I realize that I alone am responsible for them, and I am the one who must confront them."

45. What was contained in the forty-page federal complaint drafted for Laura Hamilton against her former boss William Kennedy Smith (aka "Dr. Smith") that led to his reportedly paying her a six-figure out-of-court settlement in 2004?

    a. Starting in 1998, Smith "showed an unusual interest in Ms. Hamilton and her personal life . . . [He] routinely questioned her about who she was dating and details about the relationship."

    b. Smith knew she was "dating a man who is an amputee and refused to call the man by name, referred to him derisively as 'that amputee,' and repeatedly demanded to know if Ms. Hamilton was still dating him."

    c. Smith "insisted on injecting himself" into Hamilton's social life, inviting himself along when she went out with colleagues after work, at which point "he consumed large amounts of alcohol, encouraged others to do so, and then engaged in inappropriate behavior, such as intimately touching female staff members."

d. Smith "frequently made lewd and inappropriate comments regarding women in the office," as when he referred to a breast-feeding mother pumping breast milk in the ladies' room as "milking her titties like a cow."

e. When she became pregnant in 2000, Smith would come into her office and "give her unwanted massages."

f. One night when she was staying at Smith's mother's "guest apartment," Smith showed up unannounced and, though she was seven months pregnant, "bullied her into having a glass of wine." He then massaged "her neck and back, and stroked her belly," and when she resisted he "inched his hand below her waist, and stuck his tongue in her ear."

g. After she gave birth, Smith "repeatedly attempted to remain in her office and observe her breast-feed her son." Occasionally he would just barge into her office while she was breastfeeding, explaining that, "since he is a physician, she should feel free to breast-feed in his presence."

h. All of the above, plus a 2002 incident during a conference in Croatia where Smith "maneuvered himself" into her hotel room and "produced and unwrapped a condom, making it clear that he had intended to have sexual intercourse with her," and fearing for her job and feeling that she "had no choice," she submitted to his "unwelcome sexual advances and felt degraded and humiliated afterward."

★ ★ ★ ★ ★

ANSWERS: 1. *a*, 2. *b*, 3. *c*, 4. *b*, 5. *c*, 6. *b*, 7. *a*, 8. *b*, 9. *b*, 10. *c*, 11. *b*, 12. *c*, 13. *b*, 14. *c*, 15. *b*, 16. *a*, 17. *c*, 18. *c, b, d, a*, 19. *e*, 20. *c*, 21. *b*, 22. *e*, 23. *c*, 24. *d*, 25. *g*, 26. *f*, 27. *h*, 28. *a*, 29. *i*, 30. *b*, 31. *a*, 32. *a*, 33. *b*, 34. *a*, 35. *c*, 36. *a*, 37. *b*, 38. *a*, 39. *c*, 40. *b*, 41. *c*, 42. *a*, 43. *b*, 44. *b*, 45. *h*.

THE SEXUAL
CONGRESS (#1)

MARK FOLEY *was a six-term Republican congressman from Palm Beach, Florida, whose tenure and presumed-to-be-successful reelection bid came to an abrupt end one Friday afternoon in September 2006.*

1. What did Mark Foley say in 2002 as he introduced a bill to ban Web sites devoted to "child modeling"?

    a. "These Web sites are nothing more than a fix for pedophiles."

    b. "They don't sell products, they don't sell services. All they serve are young children on a platter for America's most depraved."

    c. "These sites sell child erotica and they should be banned."

    d. All of the above, plus, "Where I have to draw the line is using children for the excitement of those more mature people who should know the difference and know better."

2. During a 2003 appearance on *The O'Reilly Factor*, about what scourge did Mark Foley sound off, "This is like putting a match next to a gas can. It's sooner or later going to explode and there'll be real dangerous consequences"?

    a. Lack of security at U.S. ports.

    b. Family nudist camps.

    c. Global warming.

3. Two of these quotes were uttered publicly by Mark Foley. Which eleven were e-mailed or instant-messaged privately by him during the same period of time?

    a. "Kids deserve protection. People that are under the age of eighteen need supervision by someone who will look out for them."

    b. "how my favorite young stud doing"

    c. "did any girl give you a hand job this weekend"

d. "well I have a totally stiff wood now"

e. "get a ruler and measure it for me"

f. "did you spank it this weekend yourself"

g. "where do you unload it"

h. "i always use lotion and the hand"

i. "grab the one eyed snake"

j. "good so your getting horny"

k. "Do I make you a little horny?"

l. "we may need to drink at my house so we dont get busted"

m. "I am deeply sorry and I apologize for letting down my family and the people of Florida I have had the privilege to represent."

4. How much time passed between Mark Foley's press secretary receiving a phone call from ABC News reading him excerpts from the instant messages and Mark Foley's resignation?

a. Two days.

b. Two hours.

c. Two minutes.

5. How did White House spokesman Tony Snow describe Mark Foley's correspondence with the young pages?

a. "Hot stuff."

b. "Naughty e-mails."

c. "Much ado about penises."

6. Referring to an e-mail from Mark Foley that, he told a colleague, "really freaked me out," what word did one congressional page use thirteen times in a row to describe Foley's request for a photo of the page?

a. "Sick."

b. "Creepy."

c. "Eew!"

7. What was Mark Foley's e-mail address?
  a. Maf54@aol.com.
  b. spankingitaswespeak@hotmail.com.
  c. bignhard@earthlink.net.

8. What incidents connected with his two-year molestation of thirteen-to-fifteen-year-old Mark Foley did Catholic priest Anthony Mercieca say "Foley might perceive as sexually inappropriate"?
  a. "Massaging Foley while the boy was naked."
  b. "Skinny-dipping together at a secluded lake."
  c. "Being naked in the same room on overnight trips."
  d. All of the above, plus something that happened while he was under the influence of pills and alcohol that he couldn't quite recall.

9. How did Anthony Mercieca justify his molestation of Mark Foley?
  a. "We were friends and trusted each other as brothers and loved each other as brothers."
  b. "It was not what you call intercourse . . . There was no rape or anything. . . . Maybe light touches here or there."
  c. Both of the above, plus, "He seemed to like it, you know? So it was sort of more like a spontaneous thing."

10. What did Anthony Mercieca say when asked if he had any message for Mark Foley in the wake of his resignation in disgrace?
  a. "If it's any consolation, I'll probably burn in hell."
  b. "Remember the good times we had together, you know, and how well we enjoyed each other's company. Don't keep dwelling on this thing, you know?"
  c. "I wish we'd had IMs forty years ago."

11. What did Mark Foley say in 1998 about President Clinton's involvement with Monica Lewinsky?

   a. "It's really no one's business but theirs."

   b. "It's vile. It's more sad than anything else—to see someone with such potential throw it all down the drain."

   c. "She's not really my type. I prefer someone with, you know, wood."

12. What was funny about Republican New York congressman Thomas Reynolds's indignantly saying, "Mark Foley betrayed the integrity of this institution as well as the trust of his colleagues and constituents. There is no excuse, and he needs to be held accountable"?

   a. Congress has no integrity.

   b. No one was held accountable for anything during the Bush years.

   c. Both of the above, plus the most powerful Republicans in Congress had known about Foley's predilection for years and had helped keep it covered up.

13. What was George W. Bush's nickname for Mark Foley—a nickname so droll that even Hillary Clinton was moved to observe, "That's clever"?

   a. "Follicles."

   b. "Folies Bergère."

   c. "Foleyman."

14. Which of the following was not part of Florida Democrat **TIM MAHONEY**'s successful 2006 campaign for the congressional seat abandoned by sex-scandal-plagued Mark Foley?

    a. The slogan "Restoring America's Values Begins at Home."

    b. The promise to give children "a world that is safer, more moral."

    c. The revelation that while he was conducting his sanctimonious campaign he was carrying on at least two extramarital affairs.

15. What did Tim Mahoney say when Patricia Allen phoned and said she wanted to break off their affair after learning that she was not the only woman he was cheating on his wife with?

    a. "You work at my pleasure."

    b. "If you do the job that I think you should do, you get to keep your job. Whenever I don't feel like you're doing your job, then you lose your job."

    c. "Guess what? The only person that matters is guess who? Me. Do you understand that? This is how life really is. This is how it works."

    d. All of the above, plus, "You're fired. Do you hear me?"

16. True or false? When Patricia Allen threatened to sue Tim Mahoney for sexual harassment—that also being how life really is—he told her, "Go right ahead. You'll never win."

    a. True. He then laughed maniacally, and she wasn't sure if he was joking or had lost his mind.

    b. False. He agreed to pay her $121,000 and get her a two-year job (at $50,000 per year) at the agency in charge of his campaign ads.

17. True or false? Despite Tim Mahoney's publicly confessed infidelity, his wife, Terry, stood by him throughout his ultimately losing campaign for reelection.

   a. True, though, to be sure, her smiles seemed less than genuine.

   b. False. Three days after he told the Associated Press that he'd had "multiple" affairs while avoiding details of exactly how many and with whom—"You're asking me over a lifetime? I'm just saying I've been unfaithful and I'm sorry for that," he said, pointing out that he'd done nothing illegal—she filed for divorce, calling the marriage "irretrievably broken."

ROGER JEPSEN *was a one-term Republican senator from Iowa who lost his bid for reelection in 1984, after certain details from his past were revealed. He was widely believed to have been generally stupid.*

18. What was the name of the minimally disguised brothel that Roger Jepsen filled out a membership application for in 1977 and paid for by credit card?

   a. Leisure Spa.

   b. Massage This.

   c. Whores 'n' Things.

19. What was Roger Jepsen's explanation for why the whole thing was really no big deal?

   a. He only went once, "in a moment of weakness."

   b. He was under the mistaken impression that the place was a "health club," though, in truth, most health clubs don't have application forms that read, "We offer nude modeling, nude encounters and nude rap sessions to our members. There are many options available that members may wish to do and it is the responsibility of the member to ask what he can do."

   c. Both of the above, and besides it happened before his "commitment to Christ" so it really doesn't count.

20. What did an anti-Jepsen campaign button say?
  a. "Roger Jepsen—Porn Again."
  b. "Roger, Over and Out."
  c. "Jepsen: Ignorance Is Bliss"

21. What did Roger Jepsen say as he launched into a speech on the Senate floor on behalf of a bill he was sponsoring?
  a. "I don't want to sound hysterical, but this is a matter of life and death."
  b. "For each of you who votes for this bill, I'll vote for one of yours."
  c. "What's in this bill, anyway?"

22. What other blunders did Roger Jepsen commit that contributed to his defeat?
  a. He made a statement that seemed to include the Methodist Church as part of a Communist conspiracy.
  b. He transferred $50,000 in campaign funds to his personal accounts.
  c. Both of the above, plus he invoked congressional immunity to avoid a ticket for using a Virginia car-pool lane while driving solo.

JOHN JENRETTE JR. *was a Democratic congressman from South Carolina who was sentenced to two years after being convicted of bribery in connection with the 1979–1980 Abscam FBI sting.*

23. According to his then wife, Rita, where in Washington, D.C., did John Jenrette and she once have sex?
  a. Atop a grave in the Confederate section of Arlington National Cemetery.
  b. In a vestibule in the National Archives.
  c. In the reflection of the Washington Monument while skinny-dipping in the Reflecting Pool.
  d. Up against the Vietnam War Memorial.

e. Under a desk in one of the Library of Congress reading rooms.

   f. In the gallery of the Supreme Court while it was in session hearing a case about pornography.

   g. In a men's room at Union Station.

   h. In the *Meet the Press* green room.

   i. Between two pillars of the Jefferson Memorial.

   j. Behind a pillar on the steps of the Capitol Building.

   k. In the Lincoln Bedroom of the White House.

   l. In Lincoln's lap at his Memorial.

   m. All of the above.

24. In which men's magazine did Rita Jenrette, alongside a nude photo layout, inform the world of that naughty tryst?

   a. *Chic.*

   b. *Playboy.*

   c. *Oui.*

25. On which TV talk show did Rita Jenrette plug that nude spread?

   a. *The Merv Griffin Show.*

   b. *The Mike Douglas Show.*

   c. *Donahue.*

26. What happened during that talk show appearance by Rita Jenrette?

   a. A female viewer called in and asked her out on a date based on the photo spread.

   b. A Hollywood agent called in to see if she was interested in pursuing an acting career.

   c. Her in-the-process-of-being-divorced husband called in and said he wanted back the $35,000 "that she took" from his checking account.

27. How did Rita Jenrette respond to that caller?

   a. She told her would-be suitor that she wasn't gay.

   b. She said she was very much interested in becoming an actor.

   c. She told John that she wanted back "my $30,000 worth of silver that you removed from the house, and every stick of furniture, and everything else you took out of the house."

28. Which films did Rita Jenrette go on to appear in?

   a. *Friday the 13th Part V: A New Beginning* and *Cannibal Holocaust.*

   b. *The Malibu Bikini Shop* and *Zombie Island Massacre.*

   c. *Porky's Revenge* and *The House on Sorority Row.*

29. On which tabloid news show did Rita Jenrette work as a "journalist" in 1989?

   a. *A Current Affair.*

   b. *Hard Copy.*

   c. *Inside Edition.*

30. Complete John Jenrette's quote as recorded by an FBI surveillance tape: "I've got _____ in my heart."

   a. thievery

   b. piracy

   c. pilferage

   d. larceny

   e. pillage

   f. banditry

   g. plunder

31. What was John Jenrette found guilty of shoplifting—and sentenced to a month in jail for—in 1988?
  a. Shirts and a watch.
  b. Shoes and a necktie.
  c. Shaving cream and a package of condoms.

Who's who?

32. Representative **JOHN A. YOUNG** (D-TX).

a. Apologized in 1978 for having "made bad judgments involving my private life" by soliciting sex from a sixteen-year-old boy and survived that scandal, only to be forced to resign his seat four years later after pleading guilty to income tax evasion and possession of marijuana.

33. Representative **FRED RICHMOND** (D-NY).

b. Was arrested in 1976 for soliciting sex from a police decoy, yet was reelected to a ninth and final term months later.

34. Representative **ARLAN STANGELAND** (R-MN).

c. Attempted in 1992 to put a positive spin on having bounced eighty-one checks through the House bank by pointing out, "It's not like molesting young girls and young boys."

35. Representative **JOE WAGGONNER JR.** (D-LA).

d. Lost his bid for a twelfth term in 1978 after former staffer Colleen Gardner said she got a raise for submitting to his sexual advances.

36. Senator **ARTHUR BROWN** (R-UT).

e. Lost his bid for an eighth term in 1990 after it was discovered that he'd made hundreds of calls to and from the home of a female lobbyist in Virginia, and about whom it was snarkily said, "[He's] a strong family man. He likes families so much that he wants to have two of them."

37. Representative **CHARLES WILSON** (D-TX).

f. Was shot in his Washington, D.C., hotel room in 1906 (and died five days later) by his longtime mistress Anne Maddison Bradley, who was pissed because she'd fathered his children, and he'd promised to marry her, and then his wife died and yet another year went by with him not setting a wedding date, and then she found letters that led her to believe that he was not only not marrying her but was also cheating on her.

JIM BATES *was a Democratic congressman from San Diego who served four terms before being narrowly defeated in 1990 by future felon Randy "Duke" Cunningham.*

38. In its 1988 story exposing the problem, which of the following did the Capitol Hill newspaper *Roll Call* cite as an example of the way Jim Bates's sexual harassment manifested itself?

  a. Bates made daily requests for hugs from his female staffers so he "would feel better" and have "more energy," during which embraces he "often patted their behinds and thanked them for being good."

b. Bates told an aide that she had "pretty lips" and inquired as to whether she'd sleep with him if they were stranded together on a desert island, to which she replied that she would not.

c. Bates stared at the breasts of one aide and said of them to the man beside him, "Yes, they do look good, don't they?"

d. All of the above, and then there was the time Bates approached an aide sitting with her legs crossed and "wrapped his legs around her extended leg, [and] began to sway back and forth, grinning, while he inquired about a specific legislative project."

39. Complete Jim Bates's apology: "The kidding around and flirting that I did, while I didn't think it was wrong at the time, I now realize was _____ "

a. very wrong; very, very wrong.

b. an egregious lapse of judgment for which I grovel for forgiveness.

c. not appropriate in some instances.

40. How did Jim Bates describe what his future behavior would be like?

a. "Much more appropriate."

b. "Much less wrong."

c. "Much like my past behavior, with the notable exception of no more hugging, groping, fondling, or ogling."

GUS SAVAGE *was a six-term Democratic congressman from Illinois' Second District. He was a total asshole long before the sex thing happened.*

41. What percentage of the recorded votes did Gus Savage miss during 1981, his first year in the House of Representatives?

   a. 22.

   b. 49.

   c. 78.

42. How did Gus Savage defend his considerable absenteeism?

   a. He said he had to deal with "a lot of personal BS."

   b. He said it was "plumb foolish to depend on legislation from a white Congress to provide for black liberation," so, in effect, none of it matters, since he's there to "agitate," not to legislate.

   c. He insisted that he'd voted 100 percent of the time and "once again the votes of the black man aren't counted."

43. In which city did Representative Gus Savage lead a demonstration of fifty thousand Communist trade unionists against American policy?

   a. Lisbon.

   b. Havana.

   c. Copenhagen.

44. What did Gus Savage call Richard M. Daley during his successful campaign for the mayoralty of Chicago?

   a. "A born-and-bred racist."

   b. "A bread-and-butter racist."

   c. "A bed-and-breakfast racist."

45. Where in Africa did Gus Savage's March 1989 indiscretion take place?
   a. Ghana.
   b. Zaire.
   c. Kenya.

46. Who was the victim of Gus Savage's indiscretion?
   a. A thirty-two-year-old hotel worker.
   b. A twenty-one-year-old State Department intern.
   c. A twenty-eight-year-old Peace Corps volunteer.

47. Where did the incident occur?
   a. In a vestibule at the U.S. embassy.
   b. In the backseat of a chauffeur-driven U.S. embassy car.
   c. In Gus Savage's hotel room.

48. According to the victim, what was the nature of the incident?
   a. "He asked me if I liked pornography, but he didn't really care what I said. He just started right in describing these graphic sex acts and asked me if I thought I might like to do them with him."
   b. "He was . . . well, let's just say he was *inappropriate.*"
   c. "He tried to force me to have sex with him. He touched me against my will. He grabbed me. He put his arms around me. He pulled me up against him. . . . He forced me to kiss him, physically forced me, pulled my mouth onto his, felt my body. . . . He was trying to lean over, get on me, lean over on me. . . . I would define it as definitely an assault. . . . He told me I was a traitor to the black movement if I didn't go along."

49. According to the victim, what was Gus Savage's response to her protests?

   a. "That's the way the world works."

   b. "I'm sixty-three. Consider this a senior citizen benefit."

   c. "Well, excu-u-u-se me."

50. How did Gus Savage avoid disciplinary action by the House ethics committee?

   a. He wrote a letter to the woman explaining that if she "felt personally offended by any words or actions of mine, I apologize, because I never intended to offend and was not aware that you felt offended at the time."

   b. He promised that "nothing like this will ever happen again."

   c. He threatened to expose similar transgressions by two other committee members.

51. What did Gus Savage say to reporters who questioned him about the incident after it became public knowledge four months later?

   a. "I don't want to talk about that. . . . Ask me the same kind of questions you ask white congressmen."

   b. "I ask you what you talk about to a grown woman in an automobile. You're grown, she's grown, and you're both single. . . . I did nothing abnormal."

   c. "I have no sexual peculiarities as some of you may have. You may be a faggot or something."

   d. All of the above, plus, "Stay the fuck out of my face. You heard what the fuck I said. Stay the fuck out of my face."

★ ★ ★ ★ ★

ANSWERS: 1. *d*, 2. *b*, 3. *b, c, d, e, f, g, h, i, j, k, l*, 4. *b*, 5. *b*, 6. *a*, 7. *a*, 8. *d*, 9. *c*, 10. *b*, 11. *b*, 12. *c*, 13. *c*, 14. *c*, 15. *d*, 16. *b*, 17. *b*, 18. *a*, 19. *c*, 20. *a*, 21. *c*, 22. *c*, 23. *j*, 24. *b*, 25. *c*, 26. *c*, 27. *c*, 28. *b*, 29. *a*, 30. *d*, 31. *b*, 32. *d*, 33. *a*, 34. *e*, 35. *b*, 36. *f*, 37. *c*, 38. *d*, 39. *c*, 40. *a*, 41. *b*, 42. *b*, 43. *a*, 44. *a*, 45. *b*, 46. *c*, 47. *b*, 48. *c*, 49. *a*, 50. *a*, 51. *d*.

LOCAL HEROES (#1)

BOB ALLEN *was a Republican state legislator who won his seat in the famous Florida election of 2000. He resigned on November 16, 2007.*

1. Whose presidential campaign was Bob Allen the Florida co-chair of when he was arrested near a public men's room on July 11, 2007, and charged with solicitation of prostitution from an undercover male police officer?
   a. Mitt Romney's.
   b. Mike Huckabee's.
   c. John McCain's.
   d. Rudy Giuliani's.

2. What did Bob Allen do that made police suspicious?
   a. He asked several people if they knew where "the guys who like to get blown hang out."
   b. He went in and out of a restroom repeatedly, almost as if he were trolling for sex.
   c. He wore a T-shirt that read, "TROLLING FOR SEX."

3. Though Bob Allen told the police, "I certainly wasn't there to have sex with anybody and certainly wasn't there to exchange money for it," how much money was he convicted of offering the cop to permit the performance of oral sex on him?
   a. $10.
   b. $20.
   c. $50.

4. What did the arresting officer say when Bob Allen asked, "I don't suppose it would help if I said I was a state legislator, would it?"
   a. "It's certainly not going to help your next campaign."
   b. "No."
   c. "It would have helped if you'd been at work voting on something instead of being here trying to blow me."

5. What was Bob Allen's explanation as to why he offered the money and servicing?

    a. He said he'd been "having sexual fantasies about Karl Rove" and that the undercover cop "reminded me of a kind of a black version of him."

    b. He said he was "doing research" for a novel he was working on about a gay legislator who liked blowing strangers in parks.

    c. He said of the undercover cop, "This was a pretty stocky black guy, and there was nothing but other black guys around in the park," and that he feared that he "was about to be a statistic" and "would have said anything just to get away." So his excuse was, he was afraid that the other black guys would beat the shit out of him, or maybe even kill him, if he didn't offer to blow the "stocky" guy—really, who hasn't been *there*? As for how he came to find himself in an area of the park habituated by gays on the prowl and surrounded by menacing African Americans, no explanation was offered.

6. True or false? Mere weeks before his arrest, Bob Allen had undergone a preliminary Scientology audit.

    a. True. After his arrest John Travolta issued a statement attesting to Allen's heterosexuality.

    b. False. There is no record of Allen being involved with Scientology. But here's something that happened weeks before he got busted: the Florida Police Benevolent Association named him "Legislator of the Year."

7. In addition to supporting the state's ban on gay adoption, what other blatant act of hypocrisy did Bob Allen engage in prior to peering twice over a men's room stall and then joining its occupant inside and telling him, "This is kind of a public place," and suggesting a brief sojourn "across the bridge," where it was "quieter"?

    a. He was an outspoken opponent of gay marriage, going so far as to decry marriages of convenience between oppositely-sexed gays.

    b. He told a Florida TV reporter that Mark Foley was "a disgrace to the state."

    c. He cosponsored a failed bill that would have increased penalties for "offenses involving unnatural and lascivious acts" (like peering twice over a men's room stall and then joining its occupant inside).

8. According to Bob Allen's lawyer, what was his client's reason for entering a park men's room five times in about an hour?

    a. He needed to relieve himself because he'd drunk too much iced tea.

    b. He needed to make some calls and that was the only spot with good reception.

    c. He was desperate for a smoke and was checking the urinals for butts.

9. What did Bob Allen *not* say in the wake of his arrest?

    a. "[I'm] the most misunderstood guy on Earth."

    b. "This is an ugly and unpleasant situation that has been thrust upon me and my family."

    c. "I was in the wrong place at the wrong time doing the wrong thing. I have no one to blame but myself."

Republican **GALEN FOX** *resigned as minority leader of the Hawaii House of Representatives in 2005, following an unfortunate run-in with the legal system.*

10. What misguided idea came to Galen Fox on December 18, 2004, during the in-flight movie on United Airlines flight 56 from Honolulu to Los Angeles?

    a. That the sleeping twenty-seven-year-old female passenger next to him was awake.

    b. That, since she was awake, the fact that she didn't remove her arm when he pressed his own arm against it on the armrest meant that "she was interested in some physical contact."

    c. Both of the above, plus the notion that since "she was interested in some physical contact," she would enjoy waking up and discovering that he had unbuckled her seat belt, unzipped her jeans, and had his hand in there.

11. Who else was on Galen Fox's flight?

    a. Johnny Depp.

    b. Senator Daniel Inouye (D-HI).

    c. The woman's parents.

12. How did Galen Fox explain his actions to the FBI?

    a. He'd noticed that the woman was lying there with her pants unzipped and he was attempting to zip them up "so no one would see her you-know" when she awoke.

    b. He'd been listening to music on his iPod that had put him "in a mood."

    c. He was trying to find a peanut he dropped into her seat.

13. In her written statement to the court, how did the victim explain her reason for pressing charges against Galen Fox?

    a. "The thought of him continuing to be respected as a public figure was too much to bear."

    b. "I brought this case forward because I had the right to sleep on a plane without being groped."

    c. "If this guy is so fond of fondling the orifices of the sleeping, let him do it in a men's jail."

14. What prompted **GLENN MURPHY JR.**—the Clark County, Indiana, Republican Party chairman and president of the Young Republican National Federation—to suddenly resign both posts in 2007?

    a. His name turned up on a list of johns in a prostitution sting.

    b. A witness came forward who said he saw Murphy with Karl Rove in a gay bar in Terre Haute.

    c. He and another man stayed overnight at someone's home after a party, and the other man woke up to find Murphy performing unsolicited oral sex on him.

15. What did Glenn Murphy say to the twenty-two-year-old man who awoke with Murphy's mouth around his penis?

    a. "This isn't what it looks like."

    b. "I thought that you were awake."

    c. "Mmmmwwwffffmmmm."

16. What did the twenty-two-year-old say to Glenn Murphy?

    a. "I don't know, dude . . . I don't know how you can possibly think that it was okay to do that, honestly."

    b. "What the fuck else could this be, dude, except what it looks like?"

    c. "Don't worry about it, dude. Who hasn't woken up to a total stranger performing fellatio?"

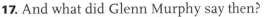

17. And what did Glenn Murphy say then?

   a. "It depends what the meaning of the word 'was' is."

   b. "Dude, I wasn't in my right mind. I wasn't thinking."

   c. "Cool. Now that you're up, could you do me?"

Who's who?

18. Maryland Public Service commissioner **CHARLES BOUTIN**.

   a. Responded in 1996 to complaints by several women that he made unwelcome advances toward them—three said he tried to kiss them—by saying, "I will say this about myself: I'm a warm, friendly person. I may have been an excessive hugger. But it was never a sexual advance."

19. New Jersey Democratic assemblyman **SILVIO FAILLA**.

   b. Followed up his stint as a state leader for Mike Huckabee's 2008 presidential campaign by becoming the third politician in a year to get caught in a local prostitution sting.

20. Minnesota Republican **PETER HONG**.

   c. Was arrested in 2008 for getting into an undercover cop's car in a gay cruise area and "attempt[ing] to manually stimulate" said cop.

21. Virginia Republican **RICHARD MIDDLETON**.

   d. Resigned in 2007 after admitting to using a state computer for sexually explicit chats with a prostitute.

22. Pennsylvania state senator **JOHN PETERSON**.

   e. Got elected to his state Senate in the mid-1960s by decrying the "moral decay of the country," then left his wife of thirty years—and their four children—to run off with his seventeen-year-old secretary.

23. Cincinnati Christian University CFO **ROBERT WILLIAMS**.

   f. Was shot to death in 1972 by a prostitute and her pimp.

JESSICA CUTLER *became the most famous $25,000-a-year Senate staffer when she posted her sex diaries on the Internet in 2004.*

24. Which senator fired twenty-four-year-old Jessica Cutler for "unacceptable use of Senate computers"?

    a. Mike DeWine (R-OH).

    b. Rick Santorum (R-PA).

    c. Jim Inhofe (R-OK).

25. Which of these descriptions of her sex partners appeared in Jessica Cutler's diaries?

    a. "'Threesome Dude.' Somebody I would rather forget about."

    b. "Serious, long-term boyfriend whom I lived with since 2001. Disastrous break up in March but still seeing each other."

    c. "The intern in my office whom I want to fuck."

    d. "My new office bf with whom I am embroiled in an office sex scandal. The current favorite."

    e. "Dude from the Senate office I interned in Jan. thru Feb. Hired me as an intern. Broke up my relationship w/QV . . ."

    f. "Lost my virginity to him and fell in love. Dude who has been driving me crazy since 1999. Lives in Springfield, IL. Flies halfway across the country to fuck me, then I don't hear from him for weeks."

    g. "Married man who pays me for sex. Chief of Staff at one of the gov agencies, appointed by Bush."

    h. All of the above, plus "A sugar daddy who wants nothing but anal. Keep trying to end it with him, but the money is too good."

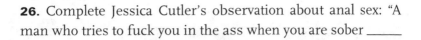

26. Complete Jessica Cutler's observation about anal sex: "A man who tries to fuck you in the ass when you are sober ____

_____"

    a. may actually be crazy.

    b. will not hesitate to have his way when you're passed out drunk.

    c. does not love you. He should at least take you out for a few drinks to spare you the pain. Now I know that [he] does not care about me, only my asshole.

27. False or true? Jessica Cutler—or, as she called herself, "Washingtonienne"—told her fellow blogger Wonkette that she was stunned at the intensity of interest in her postings.

    a. False. She said, "People are interested in sex and they're interested in politics. It's a no-brainer. How could this miss?"

    b. True. She said, "The blog is really about a bunch of nobodies fucking each other. I still can't believe people care."

28. How did Jessica Cutler justify taking money after sex?

    a. She thought of it "more like a gift than it was paying for a service."

    b. "I'm sure I am not the only one who makes money on the side this way: how can anybody live on $25K/ year??"

    c. Both of the above, but let's not dwell on this part of it, because "I don't want the IRS banging down my door."

29. What did the *Times of India* dub Jessica Cutler?

    a. The "Blog Slut."

    b. "Bonkette."

    c. The "Newinsky."

30. What did Jessica Cutler tell the *Washington Post* she planned to use her notoriety as a springboard to?

   a. An acting career, because "I'm acting every night."

   b. A career in New York book publishing, because "They'll totally hire me if I say I got fired from my job on the Hill because of a sex scandal."

   c. More sex, because "I like sex."

31. What did Jessica Cutler's notoriety actually lead her to?

   a. An acting career.

   b. A career in publishing.

   c. A job at the Manhattan escort service patronized by Eliot Spitzer.

32. What alleged behavior on the part of former California Senate leader **JOHN BURTON** prompted Kathleen Driscoll, the executive director of his San Francisco–based charitable foundation, to file a $10 million sexual harassment suit against him in 2008?

   a. He frequently had things to say about her underwear.

   b. He repeatedly commented about her breasts, as in, "Your nipples are erect."

   c. He told her she was "probably wild sexually like all Catholic girls."

   d. He told her about twenty times, "I had a dream about you last night," while raising his eyebrows suggestively.

   e. All of the above, plus he often mimicked masturbation in her presence.

★ ★ ★ ★ ★

ANSWERS: 1. *c*, 2. *b*, 3. *b*, 4. *b*, 5. *c*, 6. *b*, 7. *c*, 8. *a*, 9. *c*, 10. *c*, 11. *c*, 12. *b*, 13. *b*, 14. *c*, 15. *b*, 16. *a*, 17. *b*, 18. *d*, 19. *f*, 20. *b*, 21. *e*, 22. *a*, 23. *c*, 24. *a*, 25. *h*, 26. *c*, 27. *b*, 28. *c*, 29. *c*, 30. *b*, 31. *c*, 32. *e*.

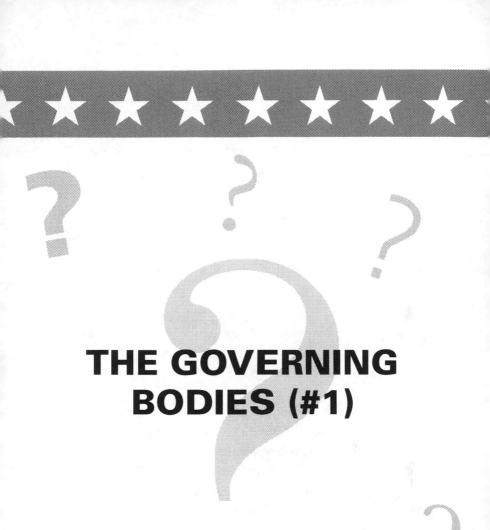

THE GOVERNING
BODIES (#1)

After threatening to run for governor of California for years, catch phrase–spouting action movie star **ARNOLD SCHWARZENEGGER** *took advantage of the short campaign attached to the 2003 recall of Gray Davis to get elected before voters had a chance to really focus on his sexual thuggery.*

1. What memory from his days as a body builder did Arnold Schwarzenegger recall fondly?
- **a.** "Once I snorted about an ounce of coke and I fucked for eighteen hours straight."
- **b.** "Once in Gold's [Gym] . . . there was a black girl who came out naked. Everyone jumped on her and took her upstairs, where we all got together."
- **c.** "Once I shot steroids right into my cock, and I fucked for eighteen hours straight."

2. What was the title of the March 2001 *Premiere* magazine article that documented various Schwarzeneggerian sexual transgressions, among them his putting his hands inside a crew member's blouse and pulling her breasts out of her bra ("I couldn't believe what I was seeing," an observer said. "This woman's nipples were exposed, and here's Arnold and a few of his clones laughing. . . . She was hysterical but refused to press charges for fear of losing her job") and his saying to a producer, upon being introduced to her ex-husband, "Is this guy the reason why you didn't come up to my hotel room last night and suck my cock?"
- **a.** "Arnold in Wonderland."
- **b.** "Arnold the Barbarian."
- **c.** "Arnold the Big Fucking Pig."

3. Five days before Republican Arnold Schwarzenegger was chosen to replace Democrat Gray Davis as governor of California, the *Los Angeles Times* published an article documenting the claims of several women who said he'd behaved grotesquely toward them over the previous three decades. Which of these accusations was included in the article?

    a. He walked up behind a nineteen-year-old at a gym, reached under her T-shirt, and touched her bare left breast with his left hand.

    b. He called a waitress he knew over to his car, said with some urgency, "Come close, it's very important," then grabbed and squeezed her left breast, and she got all teary-eyed and said, "If I was a man I would bust your jaw," and he just laughed.

    c. After doing a TV interview in a London hotel suite to promote yet another one of those moronic catch phrase–laden piece-of-shit movies of his, he told the TV host, "Before you go, I want to know if your breasts are real," so "he circled my left nipple with his finger and he said, 'Yes, they are real.'"

    d. While seated on a couch in a production office, he slipped his hand under the skirt of a secretary standing next to him. "He just held on," she said. "He held on and said, 'You have a very nice ass.' . . . I remember thinking his hand was cold on my butt . . . I was trying to figure out how to get his hand off my butt and his arm away from me without making a big deal of it. I remember thinking, 'Geez, that's a strong arm' . . . I was just thinking, 'Let me get out of here.'"

    e. He repeatedly joined a female crew member on her way down to the hotel pool and "he would pin me against the corner in the elevator" and try to take off her terrycloth robe and pull down the straps of her

Speedo, of which efforts she said, "The first time, you're like, 'Oh my God! I was groped by Arnold Schwarzenegger!' The second time you're like, 'This is disgusting.' The third time you're like, 'Get the fuck away from me.'"

f. He called out to a crew member, "Come here, you sexy devil," then pulled her onto his lap and whispered in her ear, "Have you ever had a man slide his tongue in your ass?" while all the men standing around him "were in total support mode. . . . It was kind of like everything he did was okay, and isn't it funny and isn't it swell? It was like they were proud of him. . . . Nobody said, 'What are you doing? Leave her alone.'"

g. He approached a crew member, pushed her knees apart, ground his pelvis into her for ten seconds or so, then walked away.

h. All of the above, plus he called a coffee shop waitress over to his table and "he said, a little louder than a whisper, 'I want you to do a favor for me.' I thought, okay, maybe he wanted more bread. And he said, 'I want you to go in the bathroom, stick your finger in your cunt, and bring it out to me.'"

4. Despite having dismissed the *Los Angeles Times* article as "trash politics," Arnold Schwarzenegger nonetheless had no choice—with the election five days away—but to apologize. "Yes, I have behaved badly sometimes," he said. "Yes, it is true that I was on rowdy movie sets, and I have done things that were not right, which I thought then was playful. But I now recognize that I have offended people. And to those people that I have offended, I want to say to them, I am deeply sorry about that, and I apologize because this is not what I'm trying to do." This led the waitress who was asked by Schwarzenegger to insert her finger into her vagina for him to note, "Not everyone he offended was on a movie set. I was a waitress refilling his coffee cup." But as for the behavior that did occur during filming, which studio head said, "Grabbing someone's boobs or pinching their ass is absolutely not the way people behave on a movie set. . . . No one tolerates that kind of behavior"?

   a. Paramount's Sherry Lansing.

   b. Disney's Michael Eisner.

   c. Fox's Tom Rothman.

5. True or false? There was a scene in *Terminator 3* that Arnold Schwarzenegger thought was too degrading to women, and he insisted it be removed.

   a. True. It involved a female character being groped by the Terminator, and he said he didn't understand the motivation.

   b. False. Judging from this ecstatic comment—"How many times do you get away with this? To take a woman, grab her upside down, and bury her face in a toilet bowl? I wanted to have something floating in there. . . . The thing is, you can do it, because in the end, I didn't do it to a woman. She's a machine! We could get away with it without being crucified by who-knows-what group!"—it would be hard to imagine a scene this boor would consider too degrading to women.

KIRK FORDICE *was the Republican governor of Mississippi from 1992 to 2000, during which time he twice announced his intention to divorce his wife, Pat.*

6. What happened to Kirk Fordice a year after he publicly condemned Bill Clinton for the Lewinsky affair and called on him to resign?

    a. During a White House gathering of southern governors, Clinton shook his hand and said, "Ha! I'm still here."

    b. His trip to Paris with a woman not his wife was exposed by a local TV station.

    c. His name turned up in the phone book of the prostitute known as the "Biloxi Madam."

7. What did Kirk Fordice do when a TV newsman confronted him while he was walking his dog and asked if he'd just been on vacation in Paris with a woman named Ann G. Creson?

    a. He began hyperventilating.

    b. He got all red-faced and wagged his finger and said, "Let me tell you something. You invade my privacy this way [and] six months from now I'll whip your ass."

    c. He denied even having been in Paris and said, "If you print that I was, I'll sue your ass all the way to Memphis and back."

8. Who was Ann G. Creson?

    a. Kirk Fordice's junior high school sweetheart.

    b. Kirk Fordice's best friend's wife.

    c. Kirk Fordice's wife's best friend.

9. Whose family-values-centric 2000 presidential campaign did Kirk Fordice resign as national cochairman of ten days after the campaign announced, "He is national cochairman and will remain cochairman. We are pleased to have his support"?

  a. Gary Bauer's.

  b. Alan Keyes's.

  c. Dan Quayle's.

10. How did Kirk Fordice explain that his earlier condemnation of Bill Clinton did not constitute hypocrisy?

  a. "I have never lied before a grand jury."

  b. "I have never lied to the people wagging my finger on TV."

  c. Both of the above, plus, "I have never conducted a scurrilous affair with a person half my age in the White House on public property in the middle of the day while talking [on] the telephone to a senator."

11. During his successful 2006 campaign to be governor of Nevada, Republican **JIM GIBBONS** was accused by casino cocktail waitress Chrissy Mazzeo of grabbing her, shoving her against the wall of a Vegas parking garage, and threatening her after she rebuffed his advances. Gibbons said he was gallantly walking the tipsy woman to her car when she stumbled and lost her balance, and he caught her and kept her upright. Mazzeo countered, "I was not stumbling. I did not trip. I did not need help off a wet pavement." Gibbons said he behaved like "an officer and a gentleman." Mazzeo said he was "definitely drinking and definitely aggressive [and] definitely not an officer and a gentleman," and said she'd been offered money by "the Gibbons party" to change her story and sign a statement. He said no one in his campaign offered her money to cover anything up. What "important lesson" did Gibbons say he learned from this experience?

  a. "Never to let myself be alone with a woman."

  b. "Never to offer a helping hand to anybody ever again."

  c. "Never to shove a woman against a wall and threaten her after she rebuffs me."

12. In 2008, Jim Gibbons filed for divorce, though his wife, Dawn, refused to move out of the Governor's Mansion and blamed the situation on Gibbons's "infatuation and involvement" with the wife of a Reno doctor. How many text messages to the woman—ranging from discussions of official state business to "what's happening with her kids" to "what the latest issue is with her dog"—did Jim Gibbons apologize to the citizens of Nevada for sending from a state-owned cell phone at a cost to taxpayers—later reimbursed—of $130?

   a. 374.

   b. 860.

   c. 1,300.

13. How was West Virginia governor **BOB WISE**'s affair with state employee Angela Mascia-Frye revealed in 2003?

   a. A reporter spotted them drinking together at a Charleston bar.

   b. Her husband, Philip, filed for divorce and announced that the reason was his wife was having an affair with the governor.

   c. His wife was overheard crying to a friend in a supermarket.

14. How many often-flirtatious e-mail messages between Bob Wise ("Yawn, I stayed up late last night") and Angela Mascia-Frye ("I wonder what you did staying up so late") were retrieved and released to the public?

   a. 312.

   b. 468.

   c. 541.

15. What did Philip Frye say about his cuckolding by Bob Wise?

   a. "I didn't come down with the last rain. I let this thing go on for months so I could get as much evidence as I possibly could."

   b. "I had private detectives all over this thing. I've got pictures and documents—all kinds of hard evidence."

   c. Both of the above, plus he referred to Wise as "that weasel-faced bastard. Typical Democrat."

16. Democratic Kentucky governor **PAUL PATTON** had a late-1990s affair with Tina Conner that ended badly when she broke it off and claimed he took revenge by using the powers of his office to bankrupt her business. What had her business been?

   a. She owned a catering company that had the Churchill Downs Kentucky Derby account.

   b. She owned a nursing home.

   c. She owned a chain of vintage clothing stores.

17. Despite the absence of any mainstream media reporting about it, what were the circumstances of the January 1979 death of former longtime New York governor (and former short-time appointed vice president) **NELSON ROCKEFELLER**?

   a. He choked to death on an olive when his assistant turned out not to know the Heimlich maneuver.

   b. He died of a heart attack while having sex with his assistant.

   c. He overdosed on heroin, which he'd come to late in life.

18. What was the name of the twenty-five-year-old employee/ mistress who is widely believed to have been under Nelson Rockefeller's heavy naked body when it breathed its last?

    a. Megan Marshack.

    b. Marsha Megan.

    c. Megan Marshall.

19. True or false? Liberal Republican Nelson Rockefeller's unpopularity among conservatives created a kerfuffle about whether his body would lie in state at the U.S. Capitol.

    a. True. To save face, Rockefeller's family announced that it preferred he lie in state in Albany.

    b. False. His body was cremated a mere eighteen hours after he was pronounced dead—reportedly because his wife, Happy (yes, "Happy!") didn't want an examination of the body to reveal that he'd ejaculated, since it wasn't with her.

20. While serving as governor of Louisiana in the late 1950s, Democrat **EARL LONG** had a movieworthy affair with stripper Blaze Starr. Who played Long in the 1989 movie *Blaze*?

    a. Kevin Costner.

    b. Paul Newman.

    c. Robert Redford.

★ ★ ★ ★ ★

ANSWERS: 1. *b*, 2. *b*, 3. *h*, 4. *a*, 5. *b*, 6. *b*, 7. *b*, 8. *a*, 9. *c*, 10. *c*, 11. *b*, 12. *b*, 13. *b*, 14. *c*, 15. *c*, 16. *b*, 17. *b*, 18. *a*, 19. *b*, 20. *b*.

OH, OHIO!

WAYNE HAYS *was a Democratic congressman from Ohio whose position as chairman of the House Administration Committee made him one of the most powerful figures in Washington. He served just under fourteen terms before retiring on September 1, 1976.*

1. What did Wayne Hays get for the $14,000 a year that he paid Elizabeth Ray?

    a. A devoted and fastidious worker who regularly stayed late without complaining.

    b. An invaluable sounding board on whom to test out new ideas.

    c. Sex once a week.

2. What led Elizabeth Ray to temporarily leave her job as Wayne Hays's mistress and travel to Hollywood to be an actress?

    a. Someone with very poor eyesight told her she was the "spitting image of Marilyn Monroe."

    b. She felt that she'd "been giving the Academy Award performances once a week," since her actual experience with Hays prompted her to say, "If I could have, I would have put on a blindfold, worn earplugs and taken a shot of Novocain."

    c. She'd heard that "actresses make oodles of money."

3. True or false? Wayne Hays was one of the most beloved figures on Capitol Hill.

    a. True. Shock, disbelief, and sadness were the dominant reactions to news that he had his mistress on the government payroll.

    b. False. Called "the meanest man in Congress" by Representative Phillip Burton (D-CA), Hays was almost universally despised for the spiteful ways he used his immense power as head of the House Administration Committee, and the glee that was felt at his downfall was Brobdingnagian in its scope.

4. What kind of thing, for example, did Wayne Hays do to earn such deep loathing?

    a. He resented House elevator operators sitting while he had to stand so he ordered their seats removed.

    b. He got pissed off at House barbers so he banned tipping.

    c. He controlled his colleagues' office allowances and other perks, and one can only imagine what he did with that power.

    d. He delivered vitriolic diatribes from the House floor attacking members he was unfond of, and insulted their staffers to their faces, or threatened to withhold their paychecks.

    e. He stormed into the kitchen and fired the chef in the House dining room because he wasn't happy with the hamburger he'd been served.

    f. All of the above, of course.

5. How much time passed between Wayne Hays's denial of Elizabeth Ray's claims—"Hell's fire! I'm a very happily married man"—and his admission of guilt?

    a. Three days.

    b. Two weeks.

    c. A month.

6. Why was the typewriter in Elizabeth Ray's Longworth House Office Building office unplugged?

    a. The wiring was faulty and there was a risk of fire if the sockets were overloaded.

    b. It had a three-pronged plug and the wall outlet could only accommodate two prongs.

    c. She said she had no idea how to turn it on.

7. How did Elizabeth Ray describe her assignations with Wayne Hays at her Arlington, Virginia, apartment?

a. "He is so gallant. Most times he sweeps me up and carries me into the bedroom."

b. "Every third or fourth time he comes by he cooks dinner. And he's an excellent cook."

c. "He never stops in the living room. He walks right into the bedroom and he watches the digital clock. He's home by nine-thirty."

8. What did Elizabeth Ray say Wayne Hays told her in the midst of the Wilbur Mills/Fanne Foxe scandal that he later claimed was "a figment of her imagination"?

a. "He told me that the press had 'no goddamn business worrying about who's screwing who.'"

b. "He told me that if any of his women 'ever did that to me, they'd be down there.' He pointed out the window to the Potomac. 'What do you mean, "down there"?' I said, and he looked at me and said, 'Down there, six feet under.'"

c. "He told me he'd also slept with that stripper, and that she'd told him Mr. Mills was bad in bed."

9. What prompted Elizabeth Ray to go public with the story of Wayne Hays having put her on the government payroll even though, as she told the *Washington Post*, "I can't type, I can't file, I can't even answer the phone"?

a. She was pissed off because Hays told her that she had to actually show up for work two hours a day.

b. She was upset because she hadn't been invited to Hays's wedding to another one of his secretaries, Pat Peak, for whom he'd left the wife of thirty-six years whom he was also cheating on with Ray, who said with no small pout, "I was good enough to be his mistress for two years but not good enough to be invited to his wedding."

    c. She was afraid that Hays would have her killed, because "he actually seemed nasty enough to do it, and not just do it but like doing it."

10. According to Shelley Ross in her book *Fall from Grace*, what did Wayne Hays reply when Elizabeth Ray asked him how his marriage to his secretary and former mistress would affect their relationship?

    a. "It'll make me love you all the more."

    b. "Well, I guess that'll make you Mistress Number One."

    c. "About as much as a dog burying a bone in Cleveland affects the price of milk in Seattle."

11. What was the title of Elizabeth Ray's book?

    a. *The Washington Fringe Benefit.*

    b. *Not Tonight, Dear, I Find You Repulsive.*

    c. *Can't Typecast.*

12. True or false? Editors at Dell Publishing Company, which put out Elizabeth Ray's book, said they were "surprised by what a natural writer she is."

    a. True. Her book came out three weeks earlier than planned because it required so little editing.

    b. False. One Dell employee called it a "terribly written" book by someone who was "subliterate and crazy as a coot."

13. What did Elizabeth Ray do in the aftermath of the Wayne Hays scandal?

    a. She went back to school and stunned everyone by earning a law degree from Duke University.

    b. She became a sous-chef at Duke Zeibert's.

    c. She posed nude several times for *Playboy*.

During his first year in Congress, **MARTIN HOKE** *(R-OH) only managed to make news with a politically incorrect comment to the* New York Times *about wanting to date fellow House members Maria Cantwell and Blanche Lambert because "they're hot." So, when he was approached to appear via satellite to comment on President Clinton's 1994 State of the Union address for the folks back in Cleveland, he must have seen it as a golden opportunity to finally get some good coverage.*

14. Following Clinton's speech, TV news producer Lisa Dwyer wired up Martin Hoke and his Democratic counterpart, Eric Fingerhut, then walked away, leaving them ogling her while waiting for the interview to begin. What did oblivious-to-the-fact-that-he-was-being-recorded Martin Hoke do next?

   a. He leaned over to Fingerhut and said, "I wouldn't throw her out of bed."
   b. He cupped his hands, raised them a bit, and said in a comical accent, "She has ze beeega breasts."
   c. He smacked his lips, gave Fingerhut a big grin, and said, "Me likee!"

15. True or false? Martin Hoke remained clueless about his blunder until a reporter asked him about it the next morning.

   a. True, and even then he found it hard to believe that people were making such a fuss about it.
   b. False; it was obvious from his instantly stricken look that he realized the magnitude of his blunder roughly a nanosecond after the words escaped his lips.

16. Complete Martin Hoke's fifteen-year-old daughter's observation after his ill-considered blurt had become a front-page story: "Well, Dad, _____"

   a. that was a really dumb thing to say.
   b. I'm sure Mom's friends are congratulating her for divorcing you.
   c. you just made me very proud. NOT!

17. Complete Martin Hoke's suggested penance: "I deserve
_____"

   a. to get a two-by-four to the head.

   b. no sex for a week.

   c. for everyone who ever hears my name to associate it
with that idiotic comment, as if my entire life is as
nothing compared to those two stupid seconds.

18. What was a hardly unpredictable result of the Martin Hoke
incident?

   a. Lisa Dwyer said that although she didn't hear the
remark when Hoke made it, she "was disgusted" when
she heard about it later.

   b. Outraged women-in-the-street were given an anti-Hoke
forum on local newscasts.

   c. A newspaper editorialized that Hoke failed to understand that "women who cross his line of sight are not
merely body parts assembled for his viewing pleasure."

   d. Representatives of women's groups called on Hoke "to
seek sensitivity training on gender issues."

   e. A secretary came forward and claimed that, a year earlier, Hoke had called her "a sexy little thing" and
pinched her on her thigh.

   f. Hoke said he'd sponsor a town meeting "for women
about women's issues."

   g. All of the above, plus Eric Fingerhut, who was sitting
next to Hoke when he gaffed, intoned piously, "It was
clearly an inappropriate comment. I was very uncomfortable."

19. False or true? Eric Fingerhut's sanctimonious reaction was inconsistent with his behavior at the time of the incident.

   a. False. Fingerhut's interaction with Dwyer was nothing he wouldn't happily have his wife see.

   b. True. Moments before Dwyer attracted Hoke's attention, she'd been wiring Fingerhut with a microphone, and when she asked, "Can I ask you to unbutton your jacket?" the retroactively holier-than-Hoke Fingerhut leered at her and said salaciously, "You can ask me to do anything you want." So if he truly was "very uncomfortable" with Hoke's remark, maybe it was because he was afraid his own recently uttered gaucherie would also come under unwelcome scrutiny.

20. What state office did Ohio Democrat **MARC DANN** resign from in 2008 after admitting to having had an extramarital affair with someone in his office, which admission came on the heels of the departures of several members of his staff in connection with sexual harassment charges?

   a. Lieutenant governor.

   b. Attorney general.

   c. Treasurer.

21. How many years after voting to impeach President Clinton did Ohio Republican **STEVE LaTOURETTE** call his wife to tell her he was having an affair and wanted a divorce, saying, as she quoted him, "'I want a divorce. It's over. Good-bye.'"

   a. Nine.

   b. Six.

   c. Less than five.

DONALD (BUZ) LUKENS *was an Ohio Republican whose career-long dabbling in sleaze came to fruition in 1989, during what would be his last term in Congress.*

22. How much did Representative Buz Lukens pay the teenager he had sex with in November 1988?

    a. Forty dollars, a metal pillbox, and a pink lace fan.

    b. Fifty dollars and a copy of *Appetite for Destruction*.

    c. Five dollars, but she only did it for that little because he said he could introduce her to Michael Jackson.

23. In what kind of restaurant was Buz Lukens caught on tape by Columbus TV station WSYX as he discussed with the girl's mother, Anna Coffman, his sex life with her sixteen-year-old daughter Rosie—which sex life, according to WSYX, may very well have started when Rosie was thirteen?

    a. McDonald's.

    b. Arby's.

    c. Burger King.

24. Complete Buz Lukens's explanation to Anna Coffman when she demanded to know why he'd been "messing around" with her daughter: "Well, you know, I didn't really know she was a teenager. I didn't know that, no. _____"

    a. I do now, of course.

    b. How was I supposed to?

    c. I guess you must think I'm kind of a boob.

25. True or false? To mollify Ms. Coffman, Buz Lukens pulled out a wad of cash and handed it to her.

    a. True. He then provided some unintentional comic relief by trembling so much he dropped it all over the floor.

    b. False. He did, however, offer to help her find a government job in a later phone call.

26. False or true? As his trial for contributing to the delinquency and unruliness of a minor got under way in May 1989, a Detroit TV station reported that Buz Lukens was questioned in connection with a sexual molestation case all the way back in 1954.

   a. False. It turned out to have been a case of mistaken identity.

   b. True. The case was ultimately dropped because the parents declined to press charges, but that doesn't necessarily mean he didn't do it.

27. Rosie Coffman testified that she'd "met" Buz Lukens back in 1985 and hadn't seen him again until that night in November when her nineteen-year-old friend Michelle called and said she'd "met a congressman. She called him by the name of 'Buz.'" So anyway, the two African-American girls grabbed a cab to Lukens's apartment in Columbus, and he met them at the door wearing boxer shorts and showed them to a guest room and told them to put on two black robes. According to Rosie, what did Lukens say when they asked him why they couldn't put on the white robes that were also there?

   a. "He said they were the wrong size for us."

   b. "He said they were dirty because his last whores wore them."

   c. "He said those were for white people . . . other kind of people," and that he liked "black meat."

28. False or true? After his conviction, Buz Lukens argued that Rosie Coffman's history of legal difficulties should have been admitted as evidence at the trial.

   a. False. He knew that was no excuse.

   b. True. He actually seemed to think that the girl's unvirtuousness exonerated him in some way. As Ohio state representative Michael Fox observed, "The logic of his defense is reprehensible. He's declared open season on juvenile delinquents." And as prosecutor Rita Mangini pointed out, "Her prior unruliness was not an offense in this case." And as Judge Ronald Solove said while sentencing Lukens to thirty days of actual jail time (he served nine) and a year of probation that included participation in sex offender programs and submission to testing for STDs, "This court is particularly struck by the unwillingness of the defendant to recognize that he was not the victim" and his perpetuation of the self-delusion that he was "somehow seduced by a child."

29. True or false? President George H. W. Bush said, "Next Thursday, July 20 [1989], will be an historic day for America, as America celebrates the twentieth anniversary of Neil Armstrong and Buz Lukens walking on the moon"?
- **a.** True. Buzz Aldrin was reported to have been pissed off.
- **b.** False. Dan Quayle said it, prompting the *St. Louis Post-Dispatch* headline QUAYLE PUTS SEX OFFENDER ON APOLLO II.

30. True or false? After not only refusing to resign after his conviction but also insisting on running for reelection— prompting columnist Mary McGrory to write, "[He] apparently thinks there's a constituency for older men who have sex with minors"—Buz Lukens got 17 percent of the vote in the 1990 Republican primary (so there, Mary!), and he spent the last few months of his term making no waves.
- **a.** True. He was hardly contrite, but he managed to control himself enough to stay out of the headlines.
- **b.** False. He went out in a Lukensian blaze of glory, resigning after being accused of fondling a Capitol elevator operator.

ANSWERS: 1. *c*, 2. *b*, 3. *b*, 4. *f*, 5. *a*, 6. *c*, 7. *c*, 8. *b*, 9. *b*, 10. *b*, 11. *a*, 12. *b*, 13. *c*, 14. *b*, 15. *b*, 16. *a*, 17. *a*, 18. *g*, 19. *b*, 20. *b*, 21. *c*, 22. *a*, 23. *a*, 24. *a*, 25. *b*, 26. *b*, 27. *c*, 28. *b*, 29. *b*, 30. *b*.

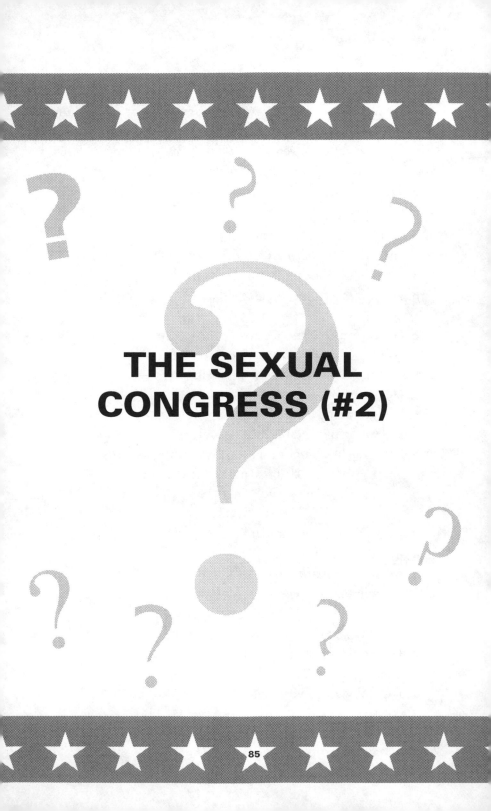

THE SEXUAL
CONGRESS (#2)

WILBUR MILLS *served in Congress from 1939 to 1977. He was the chairman of the House Ways and Means Committee from 1957 to 1975, the longest that anyone has held that post. For those eighteen years, he was one of the most powerful men in Washington. He even foolishly ran for the Democratic presidential nomination in 1972. Then some more foolish things happened.*

1. Why was Wilbur Mills's car stopped by police near the Tidal Basin in West Potomac Park on the night of October 7, 1974?

    a. He threw a beer can out of the window.

    b. His driver was speeding and didn't have his headlights on.

    c. His car was missing its rear license plate.

2. What condition was Wilbur Mills in at the time?

    a. He was high on marijuana.

    b. He was sound asleep.

    c. He was drunk and his face was all scratched up and his nose was bleeding from scuffling with Fanne Foxe, the South American stripper in the car with him, who herself had two black eyes.

3. What was Fanne Foxe's real name?

    a. Annabella Battistella.

    b. Annamaria Balastrada.

    c. Arabella Barbarosa.

4. What was Fanne Foxe's explosive stage name?

    a. The Peruvian Cherry Bomb.

    b. The Argentine Firecracker.

    c. The Bolivian Powder Keg.

5. What did Fanne Foxe do when police approached Wilbur Mills's car?

  a. She attempted to fix her hair and makeup.

  b. She ran out of the car and either jumped or fell into the Tidal Basin.

  c. She held her hands over her head and screamed, *"¡No dispara!"* (Don't shoot!) in Spanish.

6. What did Wilbur Mills do when police refused to allow him to drive Ms. Foxe home because he was drunk?

  a. He attempted to wrest the keys away from one of the cops.

  b. He shouted, "See here, I'm a congressman, and I'll have you demoted."

  c. He attempted to walk a straight line to prove his sobriety but toppled over instead.

7. False or true? So besotted with Fanne Foxe was he that a drunken Wilbur Mills once took reporter Nancy Dickerson with him to see her "perform."

  a. False. No one could be that stupid.

  b. True. Mills said of Foxe, who he is believed to have been supporting, "I own her."

8. What explosive stage name did Fanne Foxe adopt after this incident?

  a. The Potomac Pyrotechnician.

  b. The Tidal Basin Bombshell.

  c. The D.C. Detonator.

9. What was the title of Fanne Foxe's book?

  a. *The Stripper and the Congressman.*

  b. *Wilbur and Fanne: A Love Story.*

  c. *Foxe-y Lady.*

10. Despite the scandal, Wilbur Mills was reelected in November 1974. What did he do mere weeks later?
   a. He resigned his committee chairmanship.
   b. He joined Alcoholics Anonymous and checked into rehab.
   c. Both of the above, but only after showing up in Fanne Foxe's dressing room at a Boston burlesque house and boasting that he could "get her into the movies" (and that he'd written a script for her), and then drunkenly strolling onstage in the middle of her performance and then telling reporters, "This won't ruin me. Nothing can ruin me."

11. What lesson did Wilbur Mills say the Fanne Foxe affair taught him?
   a. "Never to drink champagne with foreigners."
   b. "To stay away from strippers."
   c. "If you walk out drunk onstage in a burlesque house during your stripper girlfriend's act, get ready to be seriously mocked."

12. Complete Wilbur Mills's statement: "I now believe that the fatigue   and   pressure   built   up   by   years   of _____ had an impact on me far beyond what I suspected."
   a. arrogant power-wielding
   b. drunken infidelity
   c. dedicated work for my constituents and for the whole nation

Republican **DANIEL CRANE** *was a third-term congressman from Illinois and Democrat* **GERRY STUDDS** *was a sixth-term congressman from Massachusetts when, in 1983, they made news the way no one wants to make it. Crane was defeated for reelection the following year, while Studds was reelected six more times before retiring in 1997.*

13. What did voters find out about Daniel Crane and Gerry Studds in 1983?

   a. They both rented the same porno flicks.

   b. They both had affairs with seventeen-year-old pages.

   c. They both were accused by multiple women of making unwanted advances.

   d. They both had a fetish that involved tulle.

14. What else did Daniel Crane and Gerry Studds have in common?

   a. They both were arrested for soliciting undercover cops in public men's rooms.

   b. They both turned up in the same madam's phone book.

   c. They both turned up in the same whore's tell-all book.

   d. They were both censured by the House on the same day for their errant dalliances.

15. How did Daniel Crane and Gerry Studds differ?

   a. One was conservative and one was liberal.

   b. One had been a dentist and one had been a teacher.

   c. One was from the Midwest and one was from the East Coast.

   d. One apologized for his relationship with the page and one didn't.

   e. All of the above, plus one was straight and one was the first openly gay national politician.

16. What did the *Washington Post* write about Gerry Studds's public declaration of his gayness?

   a. "On a bravery scale of one to ten, this ranks about an eight."
   b. "[It] apparently was not news to many of his constituents."
   c. "Gay, shmay! Straight, shmaight! Either way, do we really need to know?"

17. What did Daniel Crane's press secretary, William Mencarow, apologize for?

   a. Introducing the seventeen-year-old page to Crane.
   b. Telling reporters, "If they required the resignation of all congressmen who have slept with young ladies, you wouldn't have a Congress."
   c. Keeping the affair secret from Crane's wife.

18. True or false? Two weeks before his death in 2006, Gerry Studds was given an award for his tireless efforts on behalf of equality for gays.

   a. True. He was greatly moved by the ceremony and had the award in his hand when he died.
   b. False. Two weeks before he died, the Mark Foley scandal broke and the media's sudden focus on the relationships of congressmen with young pages brought the low point of Studds's career back into the public consciousness as the media embraced the opportunity to once again rehash the twenty-three-year-old story.

19. Complete adulterer Daniel Crane's statement in a National Conservative Political Action Committee fund-raising letter: "Our nation's moral fiber is being weakened by_____"
- **a.** the growing homosexual movement and the fanatical ERA pushers (many of whom publicly brag they are lesbians).
- **b.** guys who can't keep their hands off of girls young enough to be their daughters.
- **c.** keeping prayer out of the schools and putting sex education in.

20. True or false? A year before his affair with the seventeen-year-old page was made public, Daniel Crane said about rumors of a congressional sex scandal, "If they turn out to be true, I hope we'll have the maturity to deal with the transgressors with tolerance and understanding."
- **a.** True. Crane's compassion was legendary among his colleagues.
- **b.** False. What he actually said was, "If they can prove it, I hope they sock it to them and throw them out."

21. Which House member, who years later had his own scandalous sexual behavior exposed, argued that censure wasn't strong enough a punishment for offenses this serious, and that expulsion would be far more appropriate.
- **a.** Newt Gingrich (R-GA).
- **b.** Henry Hyde (R-IL).
- **c.** Bob Livingston (R-LA).

22. Complete this quote by Daniel Crane's lawyer Tom Lindley: "This does not _____"

    a. help much with any presidential ambitions he might have.

    b. fit the image Dan Crane has tried to portray.

    c. surprise anyone who knows Dan Crane.

ERNIE KONNYU *was a one-term Republican congressman from San Jose, California, who was defeated in the 1988 primary after an eventful first term.*

23. False or true? After acknowledging having asked a female aide to remove a name tag because it called attention to her breasts, Ernie Konnyu told a reporter for the *San Jose Mercury News*, "She is not exactly heavily stacked, okay?"

    a. False. Who would say something like that to a reporter?

    b. True. He explained that he'd told the aide to move the name tag "higher toward her shoulder," as it "looked inappropriate where it was parked," so it was all just a misunderstanding.

24. True or false? During her first private meeting with Ernie Konnyu, aide Michele Morse was told that she was "dressing too sexy."

    a. True. Konnyu told her he was a married man and he didn't "need any distractions."

    b. False. He told her to stop wearing flats and tailored shirts and come to work instead in high heels and frilly blouses, then had her stand up and turn around so he could "see what you look like."

25. What happened to Michele Morse?

  a. She quit.

  b. She continued to work for Konnyu through the rest of his term.

  c. She was fired, and her refusal to spend after-hours time with Konnyu is believed to have had something to do with that.

26. What happened during a lunch between Ernie Konnyu and E. F. Hutton lobbyist Polly Minor?

  a. Minor reacted badly when Konnyu's hand somehow came into contact under the table with her knee.

  b. Minor reacted badly when Konnyu asked her to stand up and turn around so he could "see what you look like."

  c. Konnyu behaved like a perfect gentleman.

VITO FOSSELLA *was a six-term archconservative New York City congressman and married father of three (and counting). Though he had been running for a seventh term, on May 21, 2008, he announced that he'd decided against seeking reelection.*

27. What happened to Vito Fossella earlier in May 2008 that led to his decision not to seek reelection?

  a. He ran a red light, and had—according to the police report—a "strong smell of alcoholic beverage."

  b. He was arrested for drunk driving after his blood alcohol level was found to be more than twice the legal limit.

  c. He told police he was rushing to take his sick daughter to the hospital, but none of the three kids he had with his wife was ill, and it turned out the child he was talking about was not one of the three kids he had with his wife but rather a fourth child, born three years earlier out of wedlock.

d. He was bailed out of the drunk tank by Laura Fay, a woman conspicuously not his wife.

e. He spent a day denying that he'd had an extramarital affair with Laura Fay that produced a child.

f. He admitted that he'd had an extramarital affair with Laura Fay that produced a child.

g. All of the above, plus he was revealed to have, essentially, two families—one back home in Staten Island with his wife, Mary Pat, and one in Virginia, with Laura Fay.

28. What, along with balancing difficulties, was one of the clues that confirmed police suspicions about Vito Fossella's lack of sobriety?

a. He misspelled his last name, leaving out one *s* and the *e*.

b. He misstated the month as "March."

c. He struggled to recite the alphabet, omitting *g* and *k*.

29. Complete Vito Fossella's apology: "My personal _____ have caused _____ to _____ and I _____"

a. failings and imperfections . . . enormous pain . . . the people I love . . . am truly sorry.

b. peccadilloes . . . some upset . . . certain people I know . . . would prefer it all hadn't happened.

c. flaws . . . humiliation . . . me and my family . . . wish I was dead.

Who's who in the way-too-long life of Dixiecrat-turned-Republican South Carolina senator **STROM THURMOND?**

30. Carrie Butler.

a. The fifteen-year-old black servant that then twenty-two-year-old Strom Thurmond had his way with in 1925.

31. Nancy Janice Moore.

b. The illegitimate daughter who resulted from the aforementioned miscegenation, who came forward with the truth at age seventy-seven, after her father finally died.

32. Essie Mae Washington.

c. The more-than-four-decades-his-junior Miss South Carolina whom then sixty-six-year-old Strom Thurmond married in 1968.

33. Which senator had the distinction of being physically accosted by ninety-year-old Strom Thurmond during a 1993 ride on a Capitol elevator?

  a. Barbara Boxer (D-CA).
  b. Carol Moseley Braun (D-IL).
  c. Patty Murray (D-WA).
  d. Dianne Feinstein (D-CA).

34. What form did this accosting take?

a. Thurmond took the woman's hand and—apparently oblivious to the fact that he was drooling—pulled it to his mouth, prompting her to yank it away and emit an involuntary noise of revulsion.

b. Thurmond put his arm around the woman, groped for her breast, and—apparently oblivious to the fact that he was talking to one of his Senate colleagues—said, "Are you married, little lady?"

c. Thurmond stood behind the woman, said, "I know you from somewhere, don't I?" and—apparently oblivious to the notion that anyone might not welcome what he was about to do—rubbed his penis against her.

35. Complete Texas senator John Tower's observation about Strom Thurmond: "When he dies, _____ _____"

a. some folks'll probably be pretty happy.

b. they'll have to beat his pecker down with a baseball bat in order to close the coffin lid.

c. it'll be hard to tell.

PAULA PARKINSON *was a farm-crop insurance lobbyist who, in January 1980, went off to Florida on a golfing weekend with three Republican congressmen. In November 1980 she appeared nude in* Playboy *in a pictorial about women in Washington called "Beauty & Bureaucracy." In March 1981 she went public with her story, a move she soon regretted.*

36. Complete Paula Parkinson's quote: "I don't do _____"

a. Democrats.

b. three-ways.

c. laundry.

37. Which congressman was not along on this golfing weekend?

    a. Representative Barry Goldwater Jr. (R-CA).

    b. Representative Tom Evans (R-DE).

    c. Representative Tom Railsback (R-IL).

    d. Representative Dan Quayle (R-IN).

38. Who was Dan Quayle?

    a. A representative from Indiana from 1977 to 1981.

    b. A senator from Indiana from 1981 to 1989.

    c. The vice president of the United States from 1989 to 1993.

    d. All of the above, and a buffoon, a simpleton, a clown who rarely expressed himself without serving up some memorable idiocy, and whose absence from the public stage in the twenty-first century is one of the few mercies shown America by an otherwise sadistic God who saw fit to send George W. Bush to destroy the nation from within.

39. Which of these men was understood by the others to be "with" Paula Parkinson on that golfing weekend?

    a. Tom Evans.

    b. Tom Railsback.

    c. Dan Quayle.

40. True or false? Representative Phil Crane (R-IL) attracted some attention by asking the Justice Department to investigate the weekend, with a particular eye toward whether any "foreign governments" were involved.

    a. False. Why would any foreign government care about a crop insurance bill?

    b. True. What a spotlight-seeking douche bag.

41. What did Dan Quayle's father, Jim, say his son majored in at college?

  a. "Broads and booze."

  b. "Quantum physics and Latin."

  c. "Big tits and bong hits."

42. According to a 1988 article in *Playboy*, Paula Parkinson told lawyers years earlier that during that infamous golf weekend, she and Dan Quayle "flirted a lot and danced extremely close and suggestively. He said he wanted to make love." How did Quayle respond to these allegations during his campaign for the vice presidency?

  a. He staged a taking-out-the-trash photo op to demonstrate what he thought of such stories, and huffily demanded "some respect and dignity for things I did not do."

  b. Not knowing that his mike was on, he laughed and told an aide, "If they really wanted to find dirt on me, they'd look at my National Guard service."

  c. He told Mike Wallace that his wife would "cut my nuts off if I even imagined it."

43. Complete the response of Dan Quayle's wife, Marilyn, to rumors that her husband had fooled around with lobbyist Paula Parkinson during a golf outing in Florida: "Anybody who knows Dan Quayle knows _____ "

  a. that *he* knows that I'd cut his nuts off if he even imagined it.

  b. he'd rather play golf than have sex any day.

  c. she's not his type. She's blonde and pretty. He likes dark, hatchet-faced women.

44. What did Paula Parkinson tell the *Washington Post* after three years of sleeping with politicians?

   a. "Sex with self-absorbed narcissists isn't all it's cracked up to be."

   b. "They're users. They're cruel, and they're certainly no better than I am. Their whole bit on their soapboxes is, 'I'm good and I'm pure and my constituents love me because I do so much good for them.' And then you get them alone . . ."

   c. "It's true what they say about the power of aphrodisiacs."

Who did what after the story about the weekend with Paula Parkinson broke?

45. Tom Railsback.   **a.** He apologized for his "association" with Parkinson and asked "my family and the Lord to forgive me."

46. Tom Evans.   **b.** He called a press conference and said he should have mentioned something to his wife about Parkinson's presence on the trip.

47. Dan Quayle.   **c.** He told reporters he barely remembered Parkinson and that he'd roomed that weekend with a male lobbyist named William Hecht and said, "I guess you might want to make something homosexual out of it."

48. All of these things happened to Tom Evans during the twenty months following the exposure of his affair with Paula Parkinson. Which of them happened last?
- **a.** His father died.
- **b.** His son told him he "screwed up" and his daughter told him she hated him.
- **c.** His best friend died of a heart attack.
- **d.** His house burned down.
- **e.** His efforts to get reelected failed.

49. Which of the following was a recollection that Paula Parkinson shared with the *Washington Post*?
- **a.** The night she arrived in Palm Beach they all went out for dinner, and they were waiting for service at the bar when she told Quayle that she was thirsty and "I had on white pants and a white sweater, and he said, 'Here, drink this,' and just picked up the pitcher of orange juice that the bartender makes screwdrivers with. So I just started drinking out of the pitcher and I remember it spilled out all over me, all over this white sweater. Everybody started laughing, tee-heeing, and then we went to dance."
- **b.** On the way to dinner one night she discovered six joints in her purse, and back home afterward she and Evans shared a laugh. "I said, 'You know, I can just see the headlines now: "Woman Lobbyist Caught in Bed with Congressman." Sex, drugs, you know, all kinds of stuff involved.' It just seemed hysterical to us."
- **c.** Both of the above, and all of it seemed much less funny when looked back on.

50. Complete Paula Parkinson's statement: "I was hurt by this whole thing, too. I still have a hard time getting jobs. It's really tough being labeled _____"
   a. a hooker.
   b. a tart.
   c. a Republican.

51. Why did Massachusetts representative **BARNEY FRANK** fire Steve Gobie, the male prostitute he'd hired (despite the man's criminal record) as his personal aide, housekeeper, and driver, in 1987?
   a. He discovered that Gobie had been stealing from him.
   b. He got tired of Gobie asking him which other congressmen were gay.
   c. He discovered that Gobie was using his apartment as a base for his prostitution business while Frank was out of town.

52. True or false? Barney Frank's insistence that Steve Gobie immediately give up all vices was a major cause of Gobie's reversion to crime.
   a. True. "It made me feel hopeless," Gobie said, "like if I couldn't be perfect I was worthless."
   b. False. Frank said he knew Gobie was still hustling when he hired him and he didn't expect him to "go cold turkey," but he figured that maybe over time the whoring would "diminish," thanks to therapy. "I thought I was Henry Higgins," Frank said of his Pygmalionesque effort.

53. Complete Barney Frank's assessment of the situation: "I don't believe it shows me as unethical. I believe it shows me as _____"

   a. gullible.

   b. nonjudgmental.

   c. optimistic.

54. True or false? When the House voted in July 1990 to reprimand Barney Frank for the Steve Gobie affair, Representative Larry Craig (R-ID) declared that he thought the whole thing was "much ado about not very much."

   a. True. Seemingly a closeted gay himself, he knew it would be best for him to tamp down the fires of homophobia, lest the winds someday blow them his way.

   b. False. In a bravura display of hypocrisy, he argued that the reprimand wasn't nearly punishment enough and voted for censure. But don't worry, he got his.

55. True or false? After he was reprimanded, Barney Frank gave several interviews in which he said he feared he would become an issue in the 1990 midterm elections.

   a. True. He felt he'd given ammunition to the enemy in the culture wars.

   b. False. He had no such fears, telling a reporter, "It is not my impression that I am on the top of people's minds across the country."

56. In 1995, Representative Dick Armey (R-TX)—himself accused of having sexually harassed his female students when he was a college professor—referred to Barney Frank as "Barney Fag." He explained it away as a slip of the tongue, saying, "I do not want Barney Frank to believe for one moment I would use a slur against him. I had a trouble with alliteration. I was stumbling, mumbling. . . . Barney Frank is a friend of mine. I don't use the word in personal conversation. I would not use such an expression and I don't approve of anyone who does this." Frank, of course, knew this was bullshit, saying, "There are various ways to mispronounce my name, but that one, I think, is the least common." To support his skepticism, Frank quoted his mother, who pointed out, "In the fifty-nine years since I married your father, no one has ever called me Elsie Fag." Five years later, Armey's homophobia flared up again. Complete the quote that he didn't even bother to pretend was accidental: "I am Dick Armey. And _____
_____"

   a. I fucking hate faggots.
   b. hey, Barney, say hi to your mother Elsie Fag for me.
   c. if there is a dick army, Barney Frank would want to join up.

★ ★ ★ ★ ★

ANSWERS: 1. *b*, 2. *c*, 3. *a*, 4. *b*, 5. *b*, 6. *b*, 7. *b*, 8. *b*, 9. *a*, 10. *c*, 11. *a*, 12. *c*, 13. *b*, 14. *d*, 15. *e*, 16. *b*, 17. *b*, 18. *b*, 19. *a*, 20. *b*, 21. *a*, 22. *b*, 23. *b*, 24. *b*, 25. *c*, 26. *a*, 27. *g*, 28. *c*, 29. *a*, 30. *a*, 31. *c*, 32. *b*, 33. *c*, 34. *b*, 35. *b*, 36. *a*, 37. *a*, 38. *d*, 39. *a*, 40. *b*, 41. *a*, 42. *a*, 43. *b*, 44. *b*, 45. *b*, 46. *a*, 47. *c*, 48. *d*, 49. *c*, 50. *b*, 51. *c*, 52. *b*, 53. *a*, 54. *b*, 55. *b*, 56. *c*.

THE PACIFIC NORTHWEST

Washington Democrat **BROCK ADAMS** *was a six-term congressman from Seattle and a member of President Jimmy Carter's cabinet before being elected to the Senate, where he served one term, at the end of which he assessed the situation, found reelection unlikely, and chose not to run.*

1. In September 1988, twenty-five-year-old Kari Tupper alleged that a year and a half earlier, Brock Adams _____ _____

    a. exposed himself to her on an almost empty D.C. subway car.

    b. made a series of late-night obscene phone calls to her in which he pretended to be another man he knew she was interested in.

    c. drugged and molested her at his home while his wife was out of town.

2. What was Kari Tupper's relationship to Brock Adams before she made her public accusations against him?

    a. She was the daughter of longtime family friends.

    b. She was a member of his Senate staff.

    c. They had no prior relationship. She was a stranger he met at a campaign fund-raising event.

3. How did Brock Adams defend himself against Kari Tupper's charges?

    a. Before she even had a chance to air them, he called a press conference and accused her of harassment and trying to extort $400,000 from him.

    b. He orchestrated a whisper campaign suggesting that she was mentally unstable.

    c. Both of the above, plus he emphatically denied all charges and had his friends issue statements of disbelief that he could have done such a thing, though his old pals the Tuppers were considerably less incredulous.

4. Though the D.C. police officer who investigated Kari Tupper's claims felt that they justified a warrant for Brock Adams's arrest, no criminal charges were ultimately filed. Over the course of the next four years, dozens of other women came forward and accused Adams of sexual misconduct ranging from forced kissing to uninvited grabbing and fondling (of breasts, thighs, and buttocks) to actual rape. How many of these women were willing to sign statements affirming their charges and testify against him in public if it came to that (which it didn't)?

   a. Three.
   b. Eight.
   c. Eleven.

5. What was Brock Adams's usual modus operandi toward his victims?

   a. He drugged their drinks.
   b. He told them tales of abuse he'd suffered as a child in an effort to evoke their pity.
   c. He offered to let them "stroke it."

6. One of Brock Adams's victims, a former secretary, told the *Seattle Times,* "One receptionist came to my office crying because she couldn't stand him touching her anymore. He was such a nuisance, it became common knowledge around the office." How did she say the staff referred to his pattern of sexual aggressiveness, which pattern the staff helped to keep secret?

   a. "Brock's brass balls."
   b. "Brock's problem."
   c. "Brock's insane notion that anyone he's attracted to must welcome his gross advances."

7. What happened when Brock Adams invited an aide to dinner to discuss political strategy?

    a. Nothing sexual; they merely ate food and talked politics.

    b. The aide confronted Adams about his unwanted sexual advances and was fired the next day.

    c. Adams coerced her into going to his apartment, where he took off his shoes and commenced to rub her leg with his feet.

8. When a reporter confronted Brock Adams at a fund-raising event and questioned him about the allegations against him, his wife, Betty, declared, "You know, we are really tired of all this scum-bum kind of stuff." What was her explanation for the plethora of sexual harassment charges against her husband?

    a. Supporters of Slade Gorton, the man whose Senate seat Adams won in 1986, had concocted the whole thing as payback.

    b. All of the accusers were members of a local coven of witches.

    c. He's physically affectionate, and some people could very well have misinterpreted that behavior, though she didn't address the question of exactly how his placing his hand firmly on another woman's upper thigh for fifteen minutes under a dinner table and resisting all efforts by the woman to pry it off could be misunderstood. Wonder what he actually meant by that.

9. How did Democrat **NEIL GOLDSCHMIDT** meet the fourteen-year-old girl he began an at-least-nine-months-and-maybe-as-much-as-three-years-long sexual relationship with in 1975, when he was the thirty-five-year-old mayor of Portland?

    a. He coached a girls' basketball team she was a member of.

    b. She was the daughter of a neighbor who'd worked on his mayoral campaign and she babysat for his young children.

    c. She sold him pot.

10. In addition to a term as governor of Oregon, what other government position did Neil Goldschmidt hold—a position also held, oddly enough, by Brock Adams—during the twenty-nine-year-period between the commencement of his sex with a fourteen-year-old and the 2004 revelation of that relationship that abruptly ended his public career with a sickening crash?

    a. U.S. Secretary of Transportation.

    b. U.S. Secretary of Commerce.

    c. U.S. Secretary of Labor.

11. Why did Neil Goldschmidt not serve time in jail for what amounted, under Oregon law, to third-degree rape?

    a. The woman chose not to press charges when the story became public.

    b. The statute of limitations had run out.

    c. He pulled a Polanski and moved to France.

Who's who in Goldschmidtworld?

12. Emanuel Rose.

a. The investigative reporter for *Willamette Week* who won the Pulitzer Prize for exposing Goldschmidt's behavior.

13. Robert K. Burtchaell.

b. The sheriff who admitted having known about the abuse.

14. Nigel Jaquiss.

c. The local businessman who helped keep Goldschmidt's, er, indiscretion a secret.

15. Bernie Giusto.

d. The rabbi who made a public appeal for forgiveness for—or at least the cessation of obsessing about—Goldschmidt.

16. While confessing in 2004 to having had an ongoing sexual relationship with a fourteen-year-old, what did Neil Goldschmidt say about the many other rumors of extramarital activity that had swirled around him throughout his public life?

a. "This was a one-time thing. Except for that youthful indiscretion, I've been as faithful as a Yellowstone geyser."

b. "If people work hard enough, I think you'll find indiscretions, but nothing as ugly as this."

c. "You know how they say, 'Where there's smoke, there's fire'? Well, there have been a few conflagrations along the way."

Senator **BOB PACKWOOD**'s *reputation as a women's rights advocate was replaced, a few weeks after his reelection to a fifth term, by a reputation as a guy who shoves his tongue inside your mouth. As one of his former aides told a reporter, "I cannot tell you how many people* *sat down with him and said, 'You are going to come to a bad end. All your career's work on women's issues . . . is going to turn to dust.'"*

17. In November 1992 the *Washington Post* broke the story of Bob Packwood's propensity for forcing himself on women. Which of these incidents was reported by one of the ten victims who came forward to recount their experiences?

    a. Packwood walked up behind a woman, kissed her on the back of the neck, was told, "Don't you ever do that again," then followed her into the next room and stood on her toes to keep her from escaping as he struggled vainly to pull off her girdle.

    b. Packwood lured a woman to his motel room, where he chased her around a table and managed to plant a kiss on her.

    c. Packwood locked the door of his office behind a woman and suddenly embraced her, running his fingers through her hair and kissing her hard on the lips before she managed to escape his clutches.

    d. Packwood was walking down a Senate corridor with a woman, then suddenly opened a door and ushered her into the room, shut the door, kissed her, and began pushing the pillows off a sofa when she pulled away.

    e. Packwood invited a woman into his office, offered her some wine (she refused), offered her a seat (she accepted), invited her to sit closer to him (she refused), then "walked over to me and pulled me out of the chair, put his arm around me and tried to kiss me. He stuck his tongue in my mouth" before she squirmed out of his grasp.

    f. All of the above, plus once he pulled out a binder and subjected a woman to his reading of several sexually explicit jokes.

18. "I have no idea why this man thinks women are going to suddenly rip their clothes off," said one of the dozen-plus more women who, in the wake of the initial revelations, came forward with their own stories of being suddenly grabbed and forcibly yet passionlessly French-kissed by Bob Packwood. Which of these incidents elicited the indignant response from Packwood, "That one I do deny"?

a. A woman said when she was thirteen she was working as one of the hostesses at a political event (and, to be fair, dressed to look much older), and Packwood walked by and grabbed her ass.

b. A woman said Packwood walked her to her car, then grabbed her and stuck his tongue in her mouth.

c. A woman said Packwood leaned across a hotel's front desk and kissed her on the lips while she was processing his checkout.

d. A woman said that when she was seventeen Packwood wrote a letter of recommendation for her college applications, then insisted on bringing it by her house when no one else was home, and of course wound up in a situation where, as she recalled years later, "I could feel the tongue coming."

e. A woman said she was at a fund-raiser for Packwood when he lingered until a room emptied, then walked up to her and wordlessly and clumsily attempted an embrace.

f. A woman said she was in Packwood's office one night typing her résumé to find another job because of his unwanted advances when he came up behind her and stuck his hand inside her shirt and reached for her breast.

19. True or false? If Bob Packwood hadn't resigned from the Senate in September 1995, he would have been expelled.

- **a.** False. Expulsion is an extreme remedy rarely invoked.
- **b.** True. The Senate ethics committee had already recommended expulsion, since, in addition to all the sexual improprieties, his diaries contained evidence that he "solicited or otherwise encouraged offers of financial assistance from five persons who had a particular interest in legislation or issues that he could influence." Plus, after the diaries had been subpoenaed, he clumsily altered them, which is also known as tampering with evidence. Expulsion would have cost him his pension, so he quit.

20. As Bob Packwood's close friend Jack Faust put it, given the sheer volume and details of the accusations, "denial is not credible. There's nothing to be gained in a denial." These five apologies were issued over the course of almost three years by Packwood. Arrange them in chronological order from first to last.

- **a.** "Am I sorry? Of course. If I did the things that they say I did, am I sorry, do I apologize? Yes."
- **b.** "If any of my comments or actions have indeed been unwelcome or if I have conducted myself in any way that has caused any individual discomfort or embarrassment, for that I am sincerely sorry."
- **c.** "Most of them are people I can't remember. I've apologized to the ones I can't remember, and I've apologized for the incidents I can't recall, and I apologize again."
- **d.** "What I was apologizing for—and again, I want you to remember, Larry, at that time, the only charges were the seven that the *Washington Post* had brought up. And, of the seven, three women I didn't know. And none of the incidents did I recognize as they talked

about them. So what I apologized for—and I'm paraphrasing it, because I can't remember what the exact words were—whatever it was I did, even if I couldn't remember it, I apologized for it. And I apologize for it again tonight. If I did things I can't remember, didn't know, or to people I didn't know, I'm embarrassed and I apologize. And that's what I meant."

e. "I'm apologizing for the conduct that it was alleged that I did."

21. True or false? The thing that's most striking about all of these apologies is Bob Packwood's touching sincerity.

a. True. He even said in one of them that he was "sincerely" sorry.

b. False. What's striking about them is the way they all hold on to the possibility, however thin, that he didn't really do any of it. "If" he did the things they said he did, "if" his behavior had indeed been unwelcome, "if" he did things he can't remember . . . well, "if" he did all that, then of course he has to be sorry about it. But maybe he's innocent. After all, most of them seem to be people he didn't even remember knowing, so how likely was it, really, that he'd done all of what he was accused of, or, really, *any* of it?

★ ★ ★ ★ ★

ANSWERS: 1. *c*, 2. *a*, 3. *c*, 4. *b*, 5. *a*, 6. *b*, 7. *c*, 8. *c*, 9. *b*, 10. *a*, 11. *b*, 12. *d*, 13. *c*, 14. *a*, 15. *b*, 16. *b*, 17. *f*, 18. *a*, 19. *b*, 20. *b, e, d, c, a*, 21. b.

NOT GAY!

ROBERT BAUMAN *was a family-values-touting congressman and father of four from the Eastern Shore of Maryland. He lost his bid for a fifth term in 1980.*

1. On September 10, 1980, the Democratic majority in the House was outmaneuvered by the Republicans in a procedural vote in connection with the kerfuffle of the moment, which involved presidential brother Billy Carter's influence-peddling in Libya. (The southern Democratic presidents always seem to have a drunken doofus brother lurking around trying to cash in on the proximity to power that they've done nothing to earn and have no idea how to use.) Anyway, the Democrats were embarrassed, and Republican Robert Bauman could barely contain his glee—the *Washington Post* said he "chortled"—as he wallowed in the moment. Three weeks later, how did Bauman get his comeuppance?

   a. He sat in gum someone had placed on his seat.

   b. He came out to the parking lot and discovered that his car had four flat tires.

   c. He found himself facing misdemeanor charges of soliciting sex and paying a sixteen-year-old boy $50 to fellate him.

2. What was Robert Bauman's explanation for the circumstances that led to his arrest?

   a. He got horny, and since he happened to be at a gay bar . . .

   b. His alcoholism made him do it—you know, you're hetero, you get sloshed, and suddenly you crave dick—but the incident had happened several months earlier ("during the period of my heaviest drinking last winter"), and he'd since licked his addiction to booze, so really, what were the odds that something like that would ever happen again? Besides, as he put it, "I do not consider myself to be a homosexual."

c. He thought he was seducing a sixteen-year-old girl and had what would years later become known as a *Crying Game* moment, then decided, what the heck, let's see what *this* is like.

3. True or false? Robert Bauman's drinking was legendary among his House colleagues.
   a. True. He was regularly found passed out in his office and frequently took to the floor reeking of liquor.
   b. False. This drinking problem that he claimed was so serious that it temporarily altered his sexual preference was, astonishingly enough, unknown to his fellow congressmen.

4. Ironically, what organization had Robert Bauman been the president of when these charges were filed?
   a. The American Conservative Union.
   b. Family First.
   c. Fathers Against Gays.

5. What legislation was Robert Bauman cosponsoring at the time the charges were filed against him?
   a. A bill to kick single mothers out of the welfare system if they continued to procreate.
   b. A bill to make abortions illegal after the first trimester.
   c. An amendment to the 1964 Civil Rights Act that would allow employers to discriminate against gays with no federal penalty.

6. Which of these statements applies to Robert Bauman?

a. The Christian Voice, an ultraconservative fundamentalist group, said his voting record in the 1979 congressional session was flawless.

b. He voted to deny federal legal assistance in cases "promoting, defending or protecting homosexuality."

c. Both of the above, plus he cosponsored a bill that sought to prohibit federal funds for any program that might "denigrate, diminish or deny the role differences between the sexes," or for any group that "presents homosexuality, male or female, as an acceptable alternative lifestyle or suggests that it can be an acceptable lifestyle."

7. Complete this statement by Dr. James C. Foor, a disappointed Bauman supporter: "This is a pretty conservative district, and people really don't like _____"

a. the homosexual thing.

b. people who can't hold their liquor to such an extreme extent.

c. surprises like this.

8. What was the title of the book Robert Bauman published in 1986 after finally coming out?

a. *The Gentleman from Maryland: The Conscience of a Gay Conservative.*

b. *The Hypocrite's Guide to Homophobia.*

c. *Who Knew? Well, I Guess I Sort of Did.*

9. False or true? Though he acknowledged having been arrested in 1976 for exposing himself to an undercover officer at the Iwo Jima Memorial, and, the next year, surviving a fire at a gay movie theater, Representative **JON HINSON** (R-MS) blamed these events on alcoholism, not homosexuality, and insisted that he wasn't gay.

    a. False. He blamed them on his mother.

    b. True. He's from *Mississippi*. What else was he going to do?

10. How many months after being reelected in 1980 did Jon Hinson resign after being charged with "disorderly conduct" with a Library of Congress messenger in a House restroom?

    a. Two.

    b. Five.

    c. Eleven.

JIM WEST *was a family-values conservative whose career in Washington State politics ended with his 2005 recall from the office of mayor of Spokane.*

11. True or false? As a Washington State representative, Jim West voted in 1986 to fund the distribution of pamphlets that explained to people how to protect themselves from AIDS during sex.

    a. True. He told intimates that it was Rock Hudson's contraction of the disease that awakened him to the urgency of the situation.

    b. False. He actually voted to prevent the state from distributing such pamphlets, explaining that this kind of information was "something people go buy at dirty bookstores."

12. What was Jim West's signature issue during his years as Washington State's Senate majority leader?

    a. Opposition to gay rights.

    b. Opposition to abortion rights.

    c. Both of the above, plus he proposed legislation that would have criminalized any kind of sexual contact—not just intercourse but also "any touching of the sexual or other intimate parts of a person"—for every unmarried person eighteen or younger.

13. Complete Spokane mayor Jim West's statement after acknowledging trolling for young men on the Internet: "I don't want to go into the whole issue, but _____"

    a. nothing is black and white, it's all shades of gay, I mean, gray.

    b. the truth will come out in time.

    c. I wouldn't characterize me as 'gay.'

14. Which morning talk show host asked Jim West, "Did you ever say, Mr. Mayor, that when you were voting against some of these bills that would have given more rights to gay couples, for example, and yet you were visiting gay chat sites and having relationships with men, did you ever in your private time say, 'Man, this is hypocritical'"?

    a. Diane Sawyer.

    b. Katie Couric.

    c. Matt Lauer.

15. During an Internet chat, Jim West offered gifts, favors, and a City Hall internship to someone he believed to be an eighteen-year-old boy. Who did the man turn out to be?

    a. A computer expert employed by Spokane's *Spokesman-Review* as part of its sting operation against West.

    b. A vice officer in the Spokane police department.

    c. Florida congressman Mark Foley.

16. Closeted gay **TERRY DOLAN** founded the National Conservative Political Action Committee, whose fund-raising letters warned, "Our nation's moral fiber is being weakened by the growing homosexual movement." How did he die in 1986 at age thirty-six?

    a. An accidental gunshot wound.

    b. A South American bus plunge.

    c. AIDS.

17. True or false? Representative **ED SCHROCK** (R-VA) withdrew from his race for a third term in 2004 after being offered his own talk radio show.

    a. True. Unfortunately, the station switched to the "Jack" music format before Schrock's show ever debuted.

    b. False. He withdrew from the race after being outed by a gay activist who was repelled by his steadfast opposition to all gay rights legislation, which included ending the "Don't ask, don't tell" policy on gays in the military because, as he put it, "You're in the showers with them, you're in the bunk room with them, you're in staterooms with them. You just hope no harm would come by folks who are of that persuasion."

RICHARD CURTIS *was a two-term Republican state legislator from southwestern Washington. He resigned in October 2007, two days after declaring, "I am not gay. I have not had sex with a guy."*

18. Which of these votes was *not* cast by Richard Curtis in the Washington House of Representatives?

    a. Yes on using state dollars to provide health care for children of illegal immigrants.

    b. No on domestic partnerships for gay couples.

    c. No on a gay rights bill banning discrimination based on sexual orientation.

19. What mistake did Richard Curtis make while on an October 2007 retreat in Spokane to discuss the upcoming legislative session?

  a. He left his computer in a cab.

  b. He ordered white wine with a beef dinner.

  c. He fell asleep in his nice hotel room, allowing Cody Castagna, the porn model he'd picked up at a sex shop and brought back there and had sex with, to steal his wallet and demand $1,000 for its return, in lieu of which he threatened to expose Curtis's gay lifestyle to his wife.

20. What was Richard Curtis reportedly wearing when he engaged in oral sex at the porn shop with a man carrying a cane—nice detail, that—before rendezvousing at his hotel with Castagna?

  a. A rented tux.

  b. Nothing but a lobster bib.

  c. Red stockings and black sequined lingerie.

21. True or false? After admitting that he had sex with Castagna, Richard Curtis explained that he didn't consider himself as having paid for said sex, despite having given the young man $100, because he saw it as a loan.

  a. True, though he admitted it was unlikely that he'd be paid back any time soon.

  b. False. First he said it was money "for gas." Then he said he gave Castagna the C-note because he was merely "trying to help somebody out." In any event, he certainly wasn't paying him to have sex. That was obviously free.

22. What did Richard Curtis's constituent Wayne Adams say about the incident?

    a. "It's none of my business. I don't know why I even have to hear about it."

    b. "The way I look at it, hell, if that's what he wants to do—as long as it's not me."

    c. "You'd think given his proclivities that he'd have a more tolerant voting record."

LARRY CRAIG *was a three-term Republican senator from Idaho. In 2007 something happened that made him decide not to run for reelection to a fourth term.*

23. Which airport can boast of being the home of the men's room where Larry Craig was arrested on June 11, 2007, for coming on to the undercover cop in the next stall?

    a. Minneapolis–St. Paul International Airport.

    b. Missoula International Airport.

    c. Boise Air Terminal.

24. In which publication did the story about Larry Craig's bathroom bust first appear?

    a. The *Idaho Statesman.*

    b. Capitol Hill's *Roll Call.*

    c. *Hustler.*

25. What did Dave Karsnia do?

    a. He claimed to have had sex with Larry Craig in 2004 in a men's room in Washington, D.C.'s Union Station.

    b. He claimed that Larry Craig came on to him in 1967 when they were in college.

    c. He claimed in 1982 that when he was seventeen he snorted coke and had sex with three congressmen, prompting Larry Craig to issue a statement saying he wasn't one of them, even though no one had said he was.

d. He arrested Larry Craig, who pleaded guilty to disorderly conduct in a public men's room.

e. He denied Larry Craig's withdrawal of his guilty plea after the whole thing became public and the upside of that plea—that it would keep the whole thing from becoming public—evaporated.

26. True or false? Most heterosexual men who were wrongly accused of a homosexual act would, as Larry Craig claimed to have done, plead guilty "in hopes of making it go away."

a. True. Most straight men are secure enough in their masculinity that they wouldn't care if they were seen in the eyes of society as guilty of public solicitation in an airport men's room.

b. False. You could scour the planet and probably never find a single one not named Larry Craig who would do it.

How much time passed . . .

27. . . . Between Larry Craig's denying a gay affair he hadn't been accused of by saying, "Persons who are unmarried as I am, by choice or circumstance, have always been the subject of innuendos, gossip and false accusations," and his subsequent marriage? **a.** One month.

28. . . . Between Larry Craig's denying a man's claims of having had sex with him in a railroad men's room and his arrest for soliciting sex in an airport men's room? **b.** One year.

29. . . . Between Larry Craig's arrest and the public's finding out about it? **c.** Two and a half months.

30. How did Larry Craig respond to the allegation by a gay man that Craig "cruised" him for half an hour in a Boise REI store in 1994?

  a. "What did he say? That I 'cruised' him? What is that, some kind of gay talk?"

  b. "Once again, I'm not gay, and I don't cruise, and I don't hit on men. I have no idea how he drew that con-clusion. A smile? Here is one thing I do out in public: I make eye contact, I smile at people, they recognize me, they say, 'Oh, hi, Senator.' Or, 'Do I know you?' I've been in this business twenty-seven years in the public eye here. I don't go around anywhere hitting on men, and by God, if I did, I wouldn't do it in Boise, Idaho! Jiminy!"

  c. "It's just my bad luck to be the type of man whose lewd actions are constantly being misconstrued as inappro-priate. It reminds me of that article in *The Onion,* 'Why Do All These Homosexuals Keep Sucking My Cock?' Pardon my language."

31. Who was *not* a member of Larry Craig's barbershop quartet the Singing Senators?

  a. Trent Lott.

  b. James Jeffords.

  c. John Ashcroft.

  d. Orrin Hatch.

32. What did Larry Craig say was one of the main things that led him to enlist in the 2008 presidential campaign of Mitt Romney, who, as Craig described his reaction to the men's room incident, "not only threw me under his campaign bus, he backed up and ran over me again"?

   a. "First and foremost, he has very strong family values. That's something I grew up with and believe in."
   b. "Have you seen him? My God, he's a beautiful man. Not that I'm gay or anything, because I'm not, but anyone with a pulse would be attracted to him."
   c. "Well, I'm certainly not going to support Giuliani. Did you know he once roomed with gay men? And when I say gay men, I mean men who have sex in public bathrooms with other men rather than in bed with their wives like I do. Men who are the exact opposite of me."

33. How did Larry Craig begin the press conference at which he announced that despite having been arrested for lewd conduct in an airport men's room, and despite allegations of homosexual experiences dating back forty years, he was, in fact, "not gay," "never [had] been gay," and surely never would be gay?

   a. "Gentlemen, I assume you see this woman on my left. Let me introduce her to you. This is Suzanne. She's my *wife*! I'm *married*!"
   b. "Thank you all very much for coming out today."
   c. "Anyone who doesn't believe I'm not gay can blow me in a toilet stall."

34. Though the phrase "wide stance" will haunt Larry Craig to his grave and likely appear in the lead paragraph of his obituary, tape transcripts of the incident in which Craig's shoe made its way under the partition and next to the undercover cop's shoe show that Craig never actually said it and had been misquoted by the arresting officer. What did Craig actually say?

  a. He referred to himself as a "fairly wide guy."
  b. He called it the "Y stance," in which he extends both legs diagonally while his torso remains upright.
  c. He said he had a "really wide foot" and sometimes had trouble containing it in his own stall.

35. False or true? During Bill Clinton's 1999 Senate trial, Larry Craig said on *Meet the Press*, "The Senate certainly can bring about a censure resolution, and it's a slap on the wrist. It's a 'Bad boy, Bill Clinton. You're a naughty boy.' The American people already know that Bill Clinton is a bad boy, a naughty boy. I'm going to speak out for the citizens of my state, who in the majority think that Bill Clinton is probably even a nasty, bad naughty boy."

  a. False. A guy with as much to hide as Larry Craig would never call attention to himself like that and give his enemies such a fantastic clip to play if he ever got into trouble.
  b. True. If you watch the tape (Google "Craig Meet the Press 1999"), you'll see that he seems to be getting himself excited as he speaks, outing himself to any sentient human.

36. How did a spokesman for Larry Craig describe the unfortunate men's room incident?

  a. "A he said/he said misunderstanding."
  b. "His Waterloo. Get it? Water-*Loo*."
  c. "That . . . that thing that happened."

37. Which of these things did *not* happen?
  a. Larry Craig announced his intention to resign from the Senate.
  b. Larry Craig voted for a constitutional ban of same-sex marriage.
  c. Larry Craig voted against adding sexual orientation to the definition of hate crimes.
  d. Larry Craig voted against prohibiting job discrimination based on sexual orientation.
  e. Larry Craig resigned from the Senate.

38. True or false? Larry Craig improperly spent just over $100,000 of campaign funds on lawyers and PR agents in the aftermath of his arrest.
  a. True, but he repaid it when the Senate ethics committee noted the impropriety.
  b. False. It was just over $200,000 of campaign funds. And he never repaid it.

39. How many people arriving for the 2008 Republican National Convention in Minneapolis made a snarky remark about Larry Craig's "wide stance" as they walked through the airport?
  a. 2,523.
  b. 4,871.
  c. Of course, it's impossible to calculate, but let's surmise it was a very big number.

★ ★ ★ ★ ★

ANSWERS: 1. *c*, 2. *b*, 3. *b*, 4. *a*, 5. *c*, 6. *c*, 7. *a*, 8. *a*, 9. *b*, 10. *b*, 11. *b*, 12. *c*, 13. *c*, 14. *c*, 15. *a*, 16. *c*, 17. *b*, 18. *a*, 19. *c*, 20. *c*, 21. *b*, 22. *b*, 23. *a*, 24. *b*, 25. *d*, 26. *b*, 27. *b*, 28. *a*, 29. *c*, 30. *b*, 31. *d*, 32. *a*, 33. *b*, 34. *a*, 35. *b*, 36. *a*, 37. *e*, 38. *b*, 39. *c*.

TV LOUDMOUTHS

1. Future tabloid television show clown **JERRY SPRINGER** re-signed from the _____ City Council in 1974 after admit-ting to having hired a prostitute, a confession made necessary by the discovery of a check he'd written to a Kentucky massage parlor for its "services."

    a. Cleveland

    b. Cincinnati

    c. Columbus

Match the insufferable conservative bloviator with the employee who sued him for sexual harassment.

2. JOHN McLAUGHLIN   **a.** Linda Dean.

3. BILL O'REILLY   **b.** Andrea Mackris.

4. What did the lawsuit against John McLaughlin charge him with?

    a. Subjecting the plaintiff to "sexually degrading and of-fensive remarks and behavior."

    b. Touching the plaintiff "intimately and against her will."

    c. Both of the above, plus informing her that he "needed a lot of sex."

5. According to the lawsuit against Bill O'Reilly, what hap-pened during his unsolicited phone calls to the plaintiff?

    a. He suggested that she buy a vibrator.

    b. He bragged about all the women he'd taught to mas-turbate.

    c. He talked about what kind of sex she and he should have together, including the possibility that she and a friend should join him for a threesome.

    d. He "babbled perversely" to her while watching a porno flick.

e. All of the above, sometimes, she thought, while he was masturbating. And not a single specific allegation was refuted.

6. What book was Bill O'Reilly promoting when he had to cancel several interviews to avoid being asked about being accused of making lurid phone calls?
   a. A book about the culture wars.
   b. A memoir with a weird title.
   c. An advice book for kids.

7. True or false? The plaintiff said that when she told Bill O'Reilly that several other women had complained about his harassment, he replied, "This is all a big misunderstanding. I'm not even sure I like women."
   a. True, though he said afterward that he'd been "joking."
   b. False. She quoted him as saying, "If any woman ever breathed a word I'll make her pay so dearly that she'll wish she'd never been born. I'll rake her through the mud, bring up things in her life and make her so miserable that she'll be destroyed."

8. In the erotic fantasy that Bill O'Reilly shared telephonically with the plaintiff, where was he having sex in the shower with her?
   a. The Fox News studio.
   b. A Caribbean hotel room.
   c. His apartment while his wife was sleeping in the next room.

9. What did the foreplay in Bill O'Reilly's shower fantasy include?

   a. A loofah.

   b. A hookah.

   c. A hooker.

10. True or false? In her sexual harassment suit against Bill O'Reilly, a former Fox News producer cited a phone message in which the hypocritical moral scold talked about his fantasy of showering with her while massaging her with a loofah. Later in the message he mistakenly referred to the loofah as farfalle.

   a. True, thus summoning the decidedly nonerotic image of rubbing her body with bow-shaped pasta.

   b. False. He referred to the loofah as "falafel," thus conjuring up the even less erotic image of smearing her body with fava beans and/or chickpeas.

★ ★ ★ ★ ★

ANSWERS: 1. *b*, 2. *a*, 3. *b*, 4. *c*, 5. *e*, 6. *c*, 7. *b*, 8. *b*, 9. *a*, 10. *b*.

LOCAL HEROES (#2)

1. True or false? When **SOL WACHTLER**, the chief judge on the New York Court of Appeals and a possible Republican guber-natorial candidate, tried to end his affair with vapid socialite Joy Silverman by claiming to be dying from a brain tumor, she asked her physician for a second opinion.

    a. True, but Wachtler declined to be examined by another doctor.

    b. False. She asked her *psychic* for a second opinion.

2. What did Sol Wachtler do after his longtime mistress Joy Sil-verman—tired of waiting for him to leave his wife—took up with another man and informed Wachtler that her new beau was younger, handsomer, and made five times as much money?

    a. He spent several hours a week stalking the other man.

    b. He began smoking a lot of marijuana.

    c. He embarked on a thirteen-month-long harassment campaign that included more than fifty cards, letters, and phone calls to Silverman and culminated in an ex-tortion scheme in which, pretending—with the aid of voice disguisers and bad makeup—to be a private de-tective from Houston named David Purdy, he de-manded $20,000 in exchange for handing over a collection of embarrassing pictures and tapes.

3. False or true? Sol Wachtler (or, rather, "David Purdy") threat-ened Joy Silverman that if his financial demands weren't met, he would kidnap her fourteen-year-old daughter and "it will cost you $200,000" to get her back.

    a. False. As upset as Wachtler was, he drew the line at in-volving Silverman's daughter in the ugliness.

    b. True. Not only that, but also he sent the daughter a wrapped condom with a note that said, "P.S. I have a picture of your mother doing 'IT.'"

4. What was Sol Wachtler reported to have said to his arresting officers?

   a. "This can't be happening. Please tell me this is a dream."

   b. "Oh, my God! Oh, my God! Oh, my God, I could have been governor!"

   c. "Someday you'll get involved with a vapid social climber who expects you to leave your wife for her and you'll try to get out of it by saying you have some fatal disease and she'll find someone younger and better-looking and richer and throw it in your face and you'll get so pissed off that the need for revenge will take over your whole life, and *then* you'll understand."

5. True or false? Sol Wachtler's arrest came as no surprise to those who knew him well.

   a. True. As one longtime friend put it, "Sol was an accident waiting to happen."

   b. False. As one longtime friend put it, "If you told me that Mother Teresa was a serial killer, I would have believed it sooner than this."

6. What did Sol Wachtler's psychiatrist blame his behavior on?

   a. Alcoholism.

   b. Asperger's syndrome.

   c. Long-term ingestion of a combination of amphetamines, antidepressants, sleeping pills, and Tylenol with codeine.

7. What was the title of Sol Wachtler's book about the fifteen months he spent in prison?

   a. *After the Madness.*

   b. *Double Life.*

   c. *Purdy and Me.*

8. Twelve years before he became homeland security chief in George W. Bush's disastrous-beyond-comprehension second term, Michael Chertoff—then the U.S. attorney for New Jersey—called a press conference to announce Judge Wachtler's arrest and indictment. What did Chertoff do to make Wachtler think he was kind of a dick whose first priority was getting himself some good publicity?

   a. Though Wachtler's culpability had long been clear, he waited weeks for the best moment to arrest him.

   b. He arrested Wachtler dramatically on the Long Island Expressway instead of waiting a few minutes until he drove home.

   c. Both of the above, plus he made sure that Wachtler's arraignment was well attended by reporters and cameramen.

9. What Texas city was **HENRY CISNEROS** mayor of when, in 1987, he began his ill-fated four-year affair with volunteer campaign worker Linda Medlar?

   a. El Paso.

   b. Austin.

   c. San Antonio.

10. How did Catalina Vasquez Villalpando, treasurer of the United States in George H. W. Bush's administration, refer to Bill Clinton and his supporter Henry Cisneros during the 1992 campaign?

   a. "Two hound dogs."

   b. "Two skirt-chasers."

   c. "Two serial adulterers."

11. From which tabloid news program did Linda Medlar receive $15,000 in exchange for copies of her surreptitiously recorded phone conversations with Henry Cisneros?

  a. *Hard Copy.*

  b. *Inside Edition.*

  c. *A Current Affair.*

12. What position in Bill Clinton's cabinet did Henry Cisneros resign from in 1997, midway through a three-year investigation by independent counsel David Barrett that led to his pleading guilty to lying to the FBI about the amount of hush money he paid to his former mistress during his 1993 vetting for that cabinet position?

  a. Secretary of Health and Human Services.

  b. Secretary of Housing and Urban Development.

  c. Secretary of Education.

13. True or false? Following Henry Cisneros's plea bargain in January 1998, David Barrett continued his investigation a full three years longer—looking into ways his original investigation was the victim of obstruction of justice—until January 2001, when a departing President Clinton pardoned Cisneros, a bunch of other people, and the wildly undeserving Marc Rich.

  a. True. The six-year-long investigation wound up costing just under $9 million.

  b. False. The *eleven-year-long* investigation—far and away the longest independent counsel inquiry ever—went on until January 2006, eight years after Cisneros's plea bargain and five years after his pardon, at a cost of $22 million, and with none of its long-promised "bombshell" contents ever becoming public.

Who did what?

14. Missouri Republican **ANDREW BUHR**.

a. Resigned his position as county commissioner in 2008 after being accused of rape by a twenty-year-old man, then exonerated himself by having secretly video-taped hundreds of sexual encounters in his home, including a perfectly consensual one between him and his accuser.

15. Arkansas Democrat **ROOSEVELT DOBBINS**.

b. Was appointed by George W. Bush in 2002 to the Commission on Presidential Scholars, from which he was removed weeks later after being charged with having sex with a fourteen-year-old boy he met in a YMCA steam room.

16. Minnesota Republican **JON GRUNSETH**.

c. Resigned from the state House in 2005 and pleaded guilty to a misdemeanor harassment charge—reduced from a sex assault charge—in connection with his fondling of a seventeen-year-old's breasts.

17. Wisconsin Republican **DONALD FLEISCHMAN**.

d. Resigned his position in the state party in 2007 after being accused of enticing and fondling and giving beer and marijuana to a sixteen-year-old runaway boy who was staying with him.

18. Pennsylvania Republican **BRUCE BARCLAY**.

e. Withdrew from his gubernatorial race in 1990—saying, "Man, it's just more than I can bear"—after stories surfaced about his 1981 Fourth of July party at which, drunk and nude, he allegedly chased a thirteen-year-old girl and tried to remove her swimsuit while other adult males swam naked in the pool with other teenage girls.

19. Connecticut Republican **PHILIP GIORDANO**.

f. Was sentenced in 2003 to thirty-seven years in prison because of his sexual involvement with a prostitute, her ten-year-old niece, and her eight-year-old daughter.

TED KLAUDT *was a Republican member of the South Dakota House of Representatives who spent his eight years in office (1999–2006) mainly focusing on and cosponsoring several bills aimed at sex offenders. Guess what happened next.*

20. Five months after leaving office, how many sex-offender-type charges—including second-degree rape of his foster children and high school pages—were filed against Ted Klaudt?

    a. Eight.

    b. Fourteen.

    c. Fifteen.

21. What was Ted Klaudt's idea to help the high school girls he was raping make some extra money?

    a. He said he could help them form a band.

    b. He said he could get the answers to state-mandated tests and the girls could sell them to other students.

    c. He said they could sell their eggs to fertility clinics.

22. False or true? Ted Klaudt told the girls that, to help them make money off their eggs, he needed to perform "breast exams" and "ovary checks" to determine the viability of their eggs.

    a. False. He knew he had no medical training and was unqualified to perform such procedures.

    b. True. Eeeewwwww!

23. When all was said and done, how many years in prison was Ted Klaudt sentenced to?

    a. 28.

    b. 54.

    c. 120.

24. Oh, and here's a sweet detail. How much did Ted Klaudt weigh?

    a. 310 pounds.

    b. 435 pounds.

    c. 600 pounds.

JACK RYAN *was a Chicago millionaire with political ambitions, married to TV actress Jeri Ryan. His strong family-values stance— he wasn't just opposed to same-sex marriage, he was against civil unions of any kind—helped him win the 2004 Republican nomination to the U.S. Senate. Then something happened and he pulled out of the race.*

25. What show did Jeri Ryan play the character Seven of Nine on?

    a. *Star Trek: The Next Generation.*

    b. *Star Trek: Voyager.*

    c. *Star Trek: Enterprise.*

    d. *Star Trek: Deep Space Nine.*

26. True or false? Jack Ryan warned state Republican officials that there might be some problems if the sealed records of his divorce from actress Jeri Ryan became public.

    a. True. Nonetheless, they decided that he was such an attractive candidate that it was worth the risk.

    b. False. He assured the chairwoman of the Illinois Republican Party that those divorce records contained nothing to be concerned about.

27. Jack Ryan's winning of the Illinois Senate nomination prompted local media to get his sealed divorce records unsealed. What in particular in those records was not only something "to be concerned about," but something damaging enough to cost him the nomination?

   a. As a younger man, he'd paid for a girlfriend's abortion.
   b. He had invested in a company that produced pornographic films.
   c. He took his recognizable celebrity wife to sex clubs, including one in New York that, according to Jeri, was festooned with "cages, whips, and other apparatus hanging from the ceiling," and tried unsuccessfully to get her to have sex with him, or at least blow him, in front of strangers.

28. True or false? According to court documents, Jack Ryan was contrite after the New York sex club fiasco and swore that he was over the whole sex club thing and would never make Jeri go to one again, and he never did.

   a. True. He realized it would probably end his marriage otherwise.
   b. False. Though he did swear that he was over the whole sex club thing and would never make Jeri go to one again, he soon took her on a "romantic getaway" to Paris and brought her to, of all places, a sex club, where, she testified, "People were having sex everywhere. I cried. I was physically ill."

29. According to Jeri's testimony, what was Jack Ryan's reaction to her tears?

   a. He said her crying was "not a turn-on" for him.
   b. He prostrated himself before her and begged her to whip him.
   c. He promised that the next time they went out, they'd go someplace *she* wanted to go.

30. How did Jack Ryan defend himself against the contents of the divorce records, the release of which he called "a new low for politics"?

    a. "She says three times over eight years [of marriage] we went to places that she felt uncomfortable. That's the worst of it. I think almost any spouse would take that as, 'Gosh, if that's the worst someone can say about me after seeing me live my life for eight years . . .' then people say, 'Gosh, the guy's lived a pretty clean life.'"

    b. "There's no breaking of any laws. There's no breaking of any marriage laws. There's no breaking of the Ten Commandments anywhere. And so . . . I think it speaks very well about my character."

    c. Both of the above, plus, he predicted, "[The effects of the disclosures on his campaign are] going to go away very quickly."

31. Who replaced Jack Ryan as the 2004 Republican Senate candidate from Illinois, thus ensuring the election of Barack Obama and putting him on the path to the White House?

    a. Former Illinois governor James R. Thompson.

    b. Former Chicago Bears coach Mike Ditka.

    c. Black right-wing nut (and Maryland resident, so what the hell was he doing running for the Senate from Illinois anyway?) Alan Keyes.

32. How did San Francisco Democratic mayor **GAVIN NEWSOM** demonstrate his appreciation to his deputy chief of staff, campaign manager, and longtime friend Alex Tourk?

    a. He gave him a Prius.

    b. He gave him a huge loaf of sourdough bread in the shape of an alligator.

    c. He had an affair in 2005 with Tourk's wife, Ruby.

JEFF GANNON *was the pseudonymous White House correspon-dent for the crackpot right-wing virtual organization Talon News who one day in 2005 called unwanted attention to himself by asking George W. Bush a question at a press conference that could just as easily have been asked by Karl Rove.*

33. What was Jeff Gannon's real name, which he claimed to have stopped using because his last name is too hard to pronounce?

   a. John David Gluntz.

   b. James Dale Guckert.

   c. Jerry Don Glooberblorg.

34. What was the question Jeff Gannon asked George W. Bush that was so unbelievably suck-uppy that it was as if he'd actually climbed up Bush's rectum and was asking the question through Bush's own mouth?

   a. "Obviously, if your father had the guts to take Saddam out when he had the chance, we wouldn't be having to deal with this now. Don't you sometimes wish your father had been more like you?"

   b. "Senate Democratic leaders have painted a very bleak picture of the U.S. economy. Harry Reid was talking about soup lines. And Hillary Clinton was talking about the economy being on the verge of collapse. . . . How are you going to work with people who seem to have divorced themselves from reality?"

   c. "Wouldn't it be better for the country and the world if we could repeal the Twenty-second Amendment and you could have a third term, and maybe even a fourth and a fifth? How old would you be then? Seventy-four? Hell, make that a sixth term."

35. True or false? Harry Reid had, in fact, talked about soup lines.

    a. True. He warned that "something's coming that will make the 1930s look like the 1990s."

    b. False. He said nothing of the sort. Rush Limbaugh had satirically attributed the soup line reference to him, but the joke clearly went over Jeff Gannon's head.

36. What was the result of Jeff Gannon's fierce line of questioning?

    a. He called so much attention to himself with his brazen sycophancy that liberal bloggers started digging into his background.

    b. They didn't have to dig very far before they linked him to various homosexual escort Web sites.

    c. Both of the above, plus, of course, they found nude photos of him all over those homosexual escort Web sites.

37. What was one of the domain names controlled by Jeff Gannon?

    a. hotmilitarystud.com.

    b. sukhotcok.com.

    c. tightsphincter.com.

38. True or false? Jeff Gannon used to attend the White House press briefing and the Senate press briefing on alternate days.

    a. True, and one day a week he'd go to the House briefing.

    b. False, because he was unable to obtain credentials for the House or Senate press galleries. Only the White House let him play reporter.

39. What journalistic experience did Jeff Gannon cite to gain access to the White House press briefing?

a. He was editor of his high school newspaper.

b. He wrote freelance articles for the *Washington Blade*.

c. As a younger boy, he had a paper route.

40. Who asked, "In an era when security concerns are paramount, what kind of Secret Service background check did James Guckert get so he could saunter into the West Wing every day under an assumed name while he was doing full-frontal advertising for stud services for $1,200 a weekend?"

a. Chris Matthews.

b. Maureen Dowd.

c. Andrew Sullivan.

41. Who referred to Jeff Gannon as "Chip Rightwingenstein of the *Bush Agenda Gazette*"?

a. Jon Stewart.

b. Bill Maher.

c. David Letterman.

★ ★ ★ ★ ★

ANSWERS: 1. *b*, 2. *c*, 3. *b*, 4. *b*, 5. *b*, 6. *c*, 7. *a*, 8. *c*, 9. *c*, 10. *b*, 11. *b*, 12. *b*, 13. *b*, 14. *b*, 15. *c*, 16. *e*, 17. *d*, 18. *a*, 19. *f*, 20. *b*, 21. *c*, 22. *b*, 23. *b*, 24. *c*, 25. *b*, 26. *b*, 27. *c*, 28. *b*, 29. *a*, 30. *c*, 31. *c*, 32. *c*, 33. *b*, 34. *b*, 35. *b*, 36. *c*, 37. *a*, 38. *b*, 39. *a*, 40. *b*, 41. *a*.

THE SEXUAL CONGRESS (#3)

MEL REYNOLDS *was a one-and-three-eighths-term Democratic congressman from Chicago who defeated, then carried on in the sleazy tradition of, his predecessor Gus Savage.*

1. How did Mel Reynolds meet Beverly Heard, the five-months-under-the-age-of-consent sixteen-year-old campaign volunteer with whom he began an illegal sexual relationship in June 1992?

   a. He was cruising her high school, called her over to his car, gave her his card, then started calling her and telling her how good she'd look naked.

   b. She worked at his local video store, and he started asking her to recommend movies to him, then invited her to his office to watch them with him.

   c. She was the daughter of a friend of his.

2. False or true? Mel Reynolds blamed his legal troubles on media racism.

   a. False. He knew racism had nothing to do with his penchant for trolling for teens.

   b. True. "If I were a white congressman with the same background, would this have happened?" he asked, then answered, "I think not."

3. What was Mel Reynolds sentenced to five years in prison for?

   a. Criminal sexual assault.

   b. Solicitation of child pornography.

   c. Both of the above, plus obstruction of justice for trying to get Heard out of town when the scandal broke.

4. What did Mel Reynolds say when Beverly Heard—who was now working with police and taping her phone calls—told him she was arranging a three-way with an imaginary fifteen-year-old Catholic schoolgirl?

   a. "I haven't had a three-way in almost a week."

   b. "Did I win the lotto?"

   c. "If she's got a younger sister, she should bring her along."

5. False or true? Mel Reynolds holds a unique place in the pantheon of political sex scandals.

   a. False. Actually, everything about his case is mind-numbingly ordinary.

   b. True. His sentence was commuted by President Clinton, after which Jesse Jackson put him on the Rainbow/PUSH Coalition payroll, thus making him—according to *National Review* writer Deroy Murdock—the only congressman who had sex with a subordinate, then won clemency from a president who had sex with a subordinate, then was hired by a clergyman who had sex with a subordinate.

6. Who was three-term New York senator **ALFONSE D'AMATO** (R-NY) so in love with in 1995 that he told the press he wanted an annulment of his thirty-five-year marriage, prompting his estranged wife, Penny, to say, "An annulment. That's the craziest thing I ever heard. Maybe you ought to ask his bastard children about it"?

   a. Actress Ellen Barkin.

   b. Gossip columnist Claudia Cohen.

   c. Political activist Patricia Duff.

ALLAN HOWE *was a Democratic congressman from Utah whose expected reelection to a second term in 1976 was a casualty of an unexpected event.*

7. According to police transcripts, what did Allan Howe say when one of the undercover policewomen he was soliciting sex from asked, "How much is it worth to you?"

    a. "A hundred, maybe one twenty-five if you're good. Are you good?"

    b. "I usually go about twenty dollars."

    c. "Is there a quantity discount?"

8. What did Allan Howe do during a 1951 religious training mission that got him excommunicated from the Mormon Church?

    a. He smoked cigarettes.

    b. He drank coffee.

    c. He got a girl pregnant.

9. What was Allan Howe's explanation for why he was in Salt Lake City's red-light district in the first place?

    a. He said that a "Chicano gentleman" had told him to drive there, and that a car would be waiting there to take him to a party.

    b. He said that a "Russian guy" had told him that two of the hookers working there were actually spies for the Soviet Union.

    c. He said that a "Chinese fellow" had told him there were big bags of money just lying around waiting to be picked up.

CHARLES "CHUCK" ROBB *was the Democratic governor of Virginia from 1983 to 1986, during which time he did something that only became public in 1991, when he was serving the first of two terms in the Senate.*

10. According to a 1990 memo titled "Womanizing" that was sent to Chuck Robb by his press secretary, the senator was widely believed _____

    a. to have engaged in "oral sex . . . with at least a half dozen women."

    b. to have gotten an intern pregnant in college "and paid for her abortion."

    c. to have "an extensive collection of pornography."

11. What was Chuck Robb's response to the allegation contained in this memo?

    a. He fired the press secretary.

    b. He threw out a lot of dirty books and VHS tapes.

    c. He didn't exactly deny it, but he said very carefully that "I haven't done anything that I regard as unfaithful to my wife, the only woman I [have] had coital sex with in the twenty years we've been married."

12. In April 1991, with NBC News about to report allegations of his extramarital affair with former Miss Virginia Tai Collins back when he'd been governor of the state, Senator Chuck Robb came forward to get his version of the story out first. What was his version of the story?

    a. Yes, he was alone with her in a room at New York's Hotel Pierre, but nothing happened.

    b. Yes, he was naked while she gave him a back rub while they were alone in that room at the Hotel Pierre, but that's as far as things went.

    c. Yes, they did share a bottle of wine while she was massaging his naked body in the privacy of their New York hotel room, but that's it! Absolutely nothing else transpired between them, so he certainly hadn't been unfaithful to his wife, Lyndon B. Johnson's older daughter.

13. As told to *Playboy* a few months after Chuck Robb's effort to spin things his way, what was Collins's version of the story?
- **a.** A ten-month platonic relationship with Robb in 1983 evolved in 1984 into an eight-month sexual one.
- **b.** She enjoyed massaging naked men but didn't see anything sexual about it.
- **c.** He was so uninterested in her that she assumed he was gay.

14. Complete this sentence in Chuck Robb's letter to Virginia Democrats as he prepared to run for reelection in 1994: "I'm vulnerable on the question of _____"
- **a.** socializing under circumstances not appropriate for a married man.
- **b.** attending parties where I didn't know people were snorting coke.
- **c.** erring on the side of incaution.

15. Why was Chuck Robb reelected despite the Tai Collins scandal?
- **a.** According to polls, a large majority of voters believed Robb's improbable tales of semi-innocence.
- **b.** Voters bought Robb's line that his wife forgave him, so they should, too.
- **c.** Neither of the above. The only thing that saved him was that the Republicans put up an even less appealing candidate.

16. Who was that even less appealing candidate?
- **a.** G. Gordon Liddy.
- **b.** Oliver North.
- **c.** George Allen.

Representative **WILLIAM BRECKINRIDGE** *(D-KY) lost his bid for a sixth term in 1896 after being successfully sued for breach of promise by his former mistress, Madeline Pollard—whom he'd seduced at seventeen and subsequently convinced to give up the two children she had by him in their infancies because he feared they could be traced to him—when, following the death of his wife, he broke his promise to marry Pollard by secretly marrying his cousin instead. And all of this despite being a moral crusader given to declarations such as, "Chastity is the foundation, the cornerstone of human society" and "Pure homes make pure government."*

17. False or true? William Breckinridge's exceeding dickishness is, funnily enough, one reason Barack Obama was elected president.

    a. False. What could one asshole's century-plus-old bad behavior have to do with the country saving itself at the last minute from being victimized by more bad behavior from present-day assholes?

    b. True. Women were so repelled by Breckinridge that they worked as a group to defeat his reelection bid, then channeled their newfound political power to get themselves the right to vote, which they did, 56–49 percent, for Obama.

DON SHERWOOD *was a family-values-touting four-term Republican congressman from Pennsylvania whose bid for a fifth term failed in 2006. His troubles started two years earlier.*

18. What was sixty-four-year-old Don Sherwood doing on the afternoon of September 15, 2004, just before his twenty-nine-year-old mistress, Cynthia Ore, "jumped up," locked herself in the bathroom of his D.C. apartment, called 911, and, according to the police, reported that he "choked her for no apparent reason"?

- **a.** Giving her a back rub.
- **b.** Making her a cup of tea.
- **c.** Reading poetry to her.

19. True or false? Don Sherwood spent the night of September 15, 2004, in jail.

- **a.** True. He wasn't bailed out until late the following day, causing him to miss an important campaign event.
- **b.** False. No arrest was made because when the police arrived, Ore—who they said had no apparent neck injuries—changed her story and said nothing had happened, prompting police to observe that she "did not seem to be of sound mind."

20. How much time passed between the occurrence of the incident and the bringing of it to the public's attention by a political opponent of Don Sherwood's who distributed a copy of the police report to newspapers and TV stations?

- **a.** Two days.
- **b.** Six weeks.
- **c.** Seven months.

21. True or false? As soon as the story became public, Don Sherwood came clean and acknowledged that he and Ore had been having a five-year-long affair.

a. True. As he put it, "This won't help my marriage or my career, but the truth is the truth."

b. False. He initially denied having asked her to his apartment and said, "You meet lots of people in Washington and I had known her casually."

22. What did the *Wilkes-Barre Times Leader* say about the incident on its editorial page?

a. "Maybe there's a logical explanation for a woman in his apartment, backrubs, and the police. The people Sherwood represents deserve to hear from him."

b. "Don Sherwood apologized Tuesday for the 'pain and embarrassment' he caused his family and supporters. What Sherwood was apologizing for was left unsaid, and frankly that makes his regret shallow and unacceptable."

c. Both of the above, and also, "[Sherwood] shouldn't be championing the sanctity of 'traditional' marriage as he was making a mockery of his own."

23. What did Cynthia Ore say initially attracted her to Don Sherwood when she met him at a Young Republicans meeting in 1999?

a. His "pink, rosy skin."

b. His "big glasses."

c. Both of the above, plus, unlike so many guys in D.C. who "try to be so suave" with their "Bentleys and Ferraris, Don has a truck."

24. Complete the statement about Don Sherwood's upcoming reelection campaign by a former primary opponent, Errol Flynn: "Even though I _____"

a. have the same name as a movie star, I'm not important enough for my opinion on this to matter.

b. would never do it myself, I think the whole mistress thing is kind of cool.

c. will not raise money for Don and I will not donate to Don, I cannot imagine not voting for Don. People like me, who are Christians, are a big part of his support. And it's people like me who are going to be offended by this, but I also have to ask myself, 'What's the alternative?' I'm not going to vote for a Democrat.

25. As if the back-rub story wasn't bad enough, what other unpleasantness was alleged in Ore's $5.5 million lawsuit against Don Sherwood (which was ultimately settled out of court while keeping the terms of the settlement private, leaving many free to believe that the charges must have been true)?

a. He often mocked her slight Peruvian accent.

b. He repeatedly hit her (often in the face), pulled her hair, and choked her.

c. He made fun of his wife with her.

26. True or false? With regard to Ore's allegations, fellow Pennsylvania family-values aficionado senator Rick Santorum said Don Sherwood "should be judged as harshly as we would judge any Democrat in his place."

a. True. Santorum took a lot of heat for this, but he stood by his principles.

b. False. Santorum—whose new book, *It Takes a Family: Conservatism and the Common Good*, attacked America's "divorce culture"—urged the public to wait "until we know all the facts and we look at the job that Congressman Sherwood is doing and make decisions based on the facts and the work he's doing," which is to say, go easy on him, he's one of ours.

27. What phrase casting aspersions on Don Sherwood's character appeared on the screen during a campaign ad for his Democratic opponent, Chris Carney?
   a. "raging hypocrite"
   b. "philandering pseudo-Christian"
   c. "a woman his daughter's age"
   d. "attempting to strangle plaintiff"
   e. "Manson Family values?"

28. False or true? Don Sherwood got his wife, Carol, to write a letter to his constituents in which she said, "Perhaps Carney gets some pleasure out of hurting our family, or maybe that's what he thinks will make him a winner."
   a. False. His campaign manager urged him to do something like that, but Sherwood said he'd "already hurt her enough."
   b. True. First he humiliated his wife with the affair, then compounded the offense by using her humiliation in an ultimately futile effort to save his seat.

29. How did Don Sherwood differentiate his indiscretions from his colleague Mark Foley's phallus-focused e-mails to male congressional pages?
   a. "He did something that was illegal. I made a mistake. I had an affair."
   b. "I'm straight. He's gay."
   c. "His thing just happened. Mine is two years old."

30. False or true? George W. Bush made a personal campaign appearance for Don Sherwood—saying, "I'm pleased to be here with Don Sherwood. He has got a record of accomplishment"—during what he had earlier proclaimed to be National Character Counts Week.

    a. False. He quietly canceled the event when that grim irony was pointed out to him.

    b. True. Sweet, ain't it? As a *Washington Post* headline summed it up, "During National Character Counts Week, Bush Stumps for Philanderer."

DAVID VITTER *was elected in 1999 to the Louisiana congressional seat formerly held by Robert Livingston, who abruptly vacated it after acknowledging that he'd more than once broken his marital vows. Vitter moved up to the Senate in 2005.*

31. How did David Vitter describe marriage in a 2006 interview with the *New Orleans Times-Picayune*?

    a. "The most important social institution in human history."

    b. "The most time-consuming relationship humans engage in."

    c. "Something that two people do together, hopefully because they want to and not just because one of them got the other one pregnant."

Who's who?

32. Jeanette Maier.

    a. The "Canal Street Madam" who said David Vitter was a former client of hers who "seemed to be one of the nicest men and most honorable men I've ever met."

33. Deborah Jeane Palfrey.

    b. The "D.C. Madam" who ran the Pamela Martin and Associates escort service, in whose records David Vitter's phone number turned up, and who later committed suicide.

34. What was David Vitter talking about when he said, "I don't believe there's any issue that's more important than this one"?
  a. Preventing global warming.
  b. Fighting terrorism.
  c. Providing universal health care.
  d. Improving education.
  e. Ending world hunger.
  f. Teaching "intelligent design" in public school classrooms.
  g. Banning same-sex marriage.

35. On August 30, 2005, in the immediate wake of Hurricane Katrina, David Vitter said of the flood levels, "In the huge majority of areas, it's not rising at all. It's the same or it may be lowering slightly. . . . I don't want to alarm everybody that, you know, New Orleans is filling up like a bowl. That's just not happening." What was happening?
  a. The Louisiana Superdome was jammed with thousands of evacuees living in utter squalor.
  b. The populace was dealing with infestations of rats, fleas, and mosquitoes.
  c. People were being rescued from their rooftops by boats.
  d. All of the above, because, you know, New Orleans was filling up like a bowl.

36. What prompted David Vitter to issue a statement acknowledging his extramarital activities?
  a. Pangs of conscience.
  b. A parking ticket he received outside of a brothel.
  c. A call from *Hustler* reporter Dan Moldea, who was working on a book with the D.C. Madam, informing him that, thanks to his enormous hypocrisy, the magazine would soon be exposing Vitter's connection to her.

37. What did reporter Dan Moldea say would determine which of the D.C. Madam's clients the magazine would expose?

   a. "If no one's ever heard of them, no one needs to."

   b. "If someone hasn't been shooting off his mouth, we'll throw him back in the river."

   c. "If they can prove they're *Hustler* subscribers, we'll give them a pass."

38. False or true? Discussing the Clinton/Lewinsky ruckus in 2000, David Vitter's wife, Wendy, said, "I'm a lot more like Lorena Bobbitt than Hillary. If [my husband] does something like that, I'm walking away with one thing and it's not alimony, trust me. I think fear is a very good motivating factor in a marriage."

   a. False. She repeatedly refused to comment about Hillary and the sex scandal because she knew that there but for the grace of God went her.

   b. True, thus becoming the only Senate wife in American history to publicly conjure up the image of severing her husband's penis, though sadly it turned out to be empty bluster and there she was seven years later, not just standing next to the unsliced slimeball but even holding his hand as he delivered his obligatory public apology.

39. Which Republican senator reacted to the David Vitter story by saying, "All of us have to look at it and say that we could be next"?

   a. South Carolina's Jim DeMint.

   b. Utah's Orrin Hatch.

   c. Arizona's John McCain.

40. Which of the following statements about David Vitter is true?

  a. At public school board meetings, he is a strong supporter of prayer in public schools.

  b. He favors abstinence-only sex education.

  c. He was vociferous in his condemnation of Bill Clinton's extramarital escapades.

  d. All of the above, plus his name turned up in a lot of blog posts that also contained the phrase "diaper fetish."

41. What was reported—but never confirmed—to be David Vitter's nickname among New Orleans prostitutes?

  a. "Davey Depends."

  b. "Vitter the Shitter."

  c. "Senator Huggies."

KEN CALVERT *is a family-values-championing Republican congressman who has represented the San Clemente/Riverside region of Southern California since 1993.*

42. What was Ken Calvert doing that attracted the attention of police early on the morning of November 28, 1993?

  a. Driving erratically with his headlights off.

  b. Loitering on a street corner known for its drug deals.

  c. Receiving fellatio in his car.

43. What did Ken Calvert do when a cop approached the car he was being blown in and the blower suddenly sat bolt upright?

  a. He quickly put Little Ken back into his unzipped pants and tried to cover up with his untucked shirt.

  b. He started his car and tried to leave and had to be told three times by the cop that he'd better stop the vehicle before he complied.

  c. Both of the above, and he assured the cop that there was nothing untoward going on, explaining oh, so convincingly, "We're just talking, that's all, nothing else."

44. What was the tone of the statement Ken Calvert issued when the story became public two months later?

    a. Destined-to-be-short-lived defiance: "I should not have to tell people what I didn't do especially when *no one* has accused me of doing anything improper. I am a forty-year-old single male, and my private life shall remain private."

    b. Dismissive disdain: "If this is the kind of thing the media jackals think is important, well, I truly pity them."

    c. Rueful contrition: "It's just the kind of thing I should never have done and hope never to do again."

45. Once it became clear that nothing less than public contrition would do, what was Ken Calvert's excuse for winding up in what he called "an extremely embarrassing situation" with Lore Lindberg, a twice-convicted prostitute, and behaving in a way that "violated the values of the person I strive to be"?

    a. He'd been feeling horny all day.

    b. He was set up by the guy who was running against him in the next election.

    c. He was all upset about his father's suicide and the dissolution of his fifteen-year marriage and "was feeling intensely lonely," plus he hadn't realized that the heroin-addicted stranger whom he'd picked up in a known red-light district and who'd been blowing him in his car, apparently out of the goodness of her heart, was a whore, and anyway, since he hadn't yet paid her, no crime was committed.

46. What list compiled by a Washington watchdog group did Ken Calvert appear on?

    a. The Ten Stupidest Excuses for Bad Behavior.

    b. The Twenty Most Corrupt Members of Congress.

    c. The Fifty Shadiest Real Estate Investments.

47. True or false? Though he represented a conservative district, Ken Calvert refused to attack Bill Clinton about the Lewinsky affair because "I know too much about the frailties of the flesh to cast that stone."

   a. True. He took a lot of heat for it at the time, but felt that behaving otherwise would have been hypocritical, given that, you know, he'd been arrested a mere five years earlier for getting blown in his car by a whore.

   b. False. He took to the floor of the House of Representatives, where he piously intoned, "We can't forgive what occurred between the president and Lewinsky," as if he hadn't been arrested a mere five years earlier for getting blown in his car by a whore.

JOHN SCHMITZ *was a California state senator—and John Birch Society member—whose political career peaked in 1972 (when, as the presidential nominee of the American Independent Party, he received more than a million votes) and cratered with a surprise announcement one July day in 1982.*

48. False or true? After chairing a 1981 committee hearing on a bill he authored that would outlaw abortion, John Schmitz issued a press release headlined, SENATOR SCHMITZ AND HIS COMMITTEE SURVIVE "ATTACK OF THE BULLDYKES."

   a. False. Though his political views were extreme, personally he was never less than civil.

   b. True. The press release noted that the audience at the Los Angeles hearing was comprised of "imported lesbians [and] anti-male and pro-abortion queer groups in San Francisco and other centers of decadence," and that "the front rows of the state auditorium were filled with seas of hard, Jewish, and (arguably) female faces," among them that of "slick butch lawyeress" Gloria Allred, for which characterization Schmitz was forced to issue a public apology and pay her $20,000.

49. True or false? The abortion hearing incident resulted in John Schmitz's lionization within the upper echelons of the John Birch Society.

    a. True. There was some talk of his being in line to succeed Robert Welch as the organization's president.

    b. False. Actually he was kicked off of the board of the rabidly right-wing group for his "extremism" after, according to Welch, "too many members objected to the cheapening of this society."

50. During the first year of President Reagan's first term, John Schmitz warned that Congress's failure to enact his economic policies would so ruin the country that "the best we could hope for is a military coup," to which a shocked journalist said incredulously, "The *best* we could hope for is a *military coup?*" What was Schmitz's response?

    a. "What better way to round up all the Jews and queers?"

    b. "A good military coup. Not a bad military coup, a good military coup."

    c. "Okay, so maybe I'm given to hyperbole at times. But things would definitely be in bad shape."

51. What contributed to the end of John Schmitz's political career?

    a. He acknowledged being the father, with a former student of his, of an illegitimate child.

    b. His illegitimate child, an infant boy, was rushed to the hospital with a hair tied so tightly around his penis that it was almost severed—an unusual injury, to be sure, and one that went unexplained by the boy's mother.

    c. Both of the above, plus he acknowledged that he and his former student also had an illegitimate daughter.

52. Complete John Schmitz's statement after his extramarital paternity became public: "I ought to get _____ for this."

   a. a public spanking

   b. the Right-to-Life man-of-the-year award

   c. a vasectomy

53. True or false? John Schmitz was a rabid opponent of sex education and had been known to pull his daughter out of any school that threatened to teach it, which was amusing in retrospect because his daughter grew up to be a sex education teacher.

   a. True. She came up with a curriculum that is currently used in twenty-one states.

   b. False. It's amusing in retrospect because his non-sex-educated daughter grew up to be a thirty-four-year-old Seattle schoolteacher who had an affair—and two children—with her thirteen-year-old sixth-grade student, whom she married after getting out of jail for statutory rape. Yes! Mary Kay Letourneau!

★ ★ ★ ★ ★

ANSWERS: 1. *a*, 2. *b*, 3. *c*, 4. *b*, 5. *b*, 6. *b*, 7. *b*, 8. *c*, 9. *b*, 10. *a*, 11. *c*, 12. *c*, 13. *a*, 14. *a*, 15. *c*, 16. *b*, 17. *b*, 18. *a*, 19. *b*, 20. *c*, 21. *b*, 22. *c*, 23. *c*, 24. *c*, 25. *b*, 26. *b*, 27. *d*, 28. *b*, 29. *a*, 30. *b*, 31. *a*, 32. *a*, 33. *b*, 34. *g*, 35. *d*, 36. *c*, 37. *b*, 38. *b*, 39. *a*, 40. *d*, 41. *b*, 42. *c*, 43. *c*, 44. *a*, 45. *c*, 46. *b*, 47. *b*, 48. *b*, 49. *b*, 50. *b*, 51. *c*, 52. *b*, 53. *b*.

THE RELIGIOUS
WRONG

1. In 1987 the *Charlotte Observer* reported that televangelist **JIM BAKKER** paid $115,000 in hush money to cover up his 1980 one-time dalliance with then-twenty-one-year-old Jessica Hahn. How did they meet?

   a. She was a church secretary.

   b. She babysat for his kids.

   c. She was his wife's makeup consultant.

2. Jim Bakker claimed that Jessica Hahn knew "all the tricks of the trade," and was the aggressor in the sexual encounter that she said made her feel "like a piece of hamburger somebody threw out in the street." What was Hahn's side of the story?

   a. Her parents watched the PTL Club and she'd had a crush on Bakker since she was fifteen.

   b. She was a virgin who was raped by Bakker—and then by his friend John Fletcher—after she drank drugged wine.

   c. She was using him to get to Tammy, whom she had a crush on.

3. False or true? Tammy Faye Bakker wore makeup to bed.

   a. False. She used to joke that when she washed it off at night, it was "the fastest ten pounds anyone ever lost."

   b. True. As she explained, "Jim has very seldom seen me without makeup and hardly ever in my life without eyelashes. I think every woman ought to wear eyelashes, because I think the eyes are such an important part of the face."

4. Louisiana-based rival televangelist **JIMMY SWAGGART** initiated the investigation of the Bakker/Hahn affair. Who stepped in and took over the PTL televangelism ministry—temporarily, he said dishonestly—when Jim Bakker was forced to resign?
   a. Jimmy Swaggart.
   b. Pat Robertson.
   c. Jerry Falwell.

5. Which of these is not one of the things that PTL is known to stand for among the evangelical community?
   a. Praise the Lord.
   b. People That Love.
   c. Pass the Latkes.

6. Displaying his fundamentalist contempt for the charismatic Pentecostals who made up a significant portion of the PTL ministry, Jerry Falwell observed that people who speak in tongues _____
   a. "have been known to frighten small children, sometimes even their own."
   b. "must be used to not being understood."
   c. "ate too much pizza last night."

7. What did rival TV preacher John Ankerberg accuse Jim Bakker of?
   a. Having sex with prostitutes.
   b. Having sex with homosexuals.
   c. Condoning wife-swapping.
   d. All of the above, plus embezzling millions of dollars in ministry funds.

8. False or true? When Jerry Falwell refused to give Jim Bakker back his ministry, Jimmy Swaggart sided with Bakker.

    a. False. Falwell had promised him a piece of the pie if he sided with him.

    b. True. Swaggart feared that Falwell was becoming too powerful. "If I tell you I'm going to keep your truck for five days and then I'm going to give it back to you," he said, "and then someone finds out you're a homosexual, I still owe you your truck."

9. Five months after their scandal broke, Jim and Tammy Faye Bakker announced a "Farewell for Now" tour featuring Tammy Faye's singing and Jim's "sharing from his heart." Why was the twenty-five-city tour canceled before it began?

    a. Jim's mental state was iffy, as he was spending more and more of his time in the fetal position.

    b. Only thirty-two tickets were sold for the Nashville opening.

    c. Tammy Faye developed an allergy to mascara.

10. According to Jessica Hahn, Jim Bakker "told me Tammy was very big and that he couldn't be satisfied by her. Those were his words exactly." What else did he say to her back in December 1980 to get her to have sex with him?

    a. "But just because Tammy's too big for me doesn't mean I'm not big, too."

    b. "When you help the shepherd, you're helping the sheep."

    c. "If God didn't want you to sleep with me, he wouldn't have you here with me now."

11. What comedian did Jessica Hahn hook up with after the scandal broke?

   a. Sam Kinison.

   b. Pee-Wee Herman.

   c. Andrew Dice Clay.

12. What late-1980s video did Jessica Hahn writhe around in lingerie in?

   a. *Wild Thing.*

   b. *Here I Go Again.*

   c. *Legs.*

13. What did Tammy Faye Bakker say was the tip-off that she had a prescription drug addiction?

   a. When she was itching so much she rubbed her arms raw.

   b. When she started spending more money on drugs than on makeup.

   c. When she saw people and cats on the wing of an airplane.

14. Who referred to Jim Bakker as "the greatest scab and cancer on the face of Christianity in two thousand years of church history"?

   a. Jerry Falwell.

   b. Pat Robertson.

   c. Jessica Hahn.

15. True or false? Though Jimmy Swaggart was known for his hatred of the competition, he had a soft spot for Jim Bakker.

   a. True. He made a point of staying at the hotel at Bakker's Heritage USA theme park whenever he found himself in Fort Mill, South Carolina.

   b. False. He loathed Bakker, whom he referred to as a "cancer" on the ministry scene, and expressed his contempt for "pretty little boys with their hair done and their nails done who call themselves preachers."

16. In 1986, Jimmy Swaggart exposed rival Assemblies of God pastor Marvin Gorman's affair with another pastor's wife. In 1987, Swaggart exposed Jim Bakker's seven-year-old dalliance with Jessica Hahn. What happened in February 1988?

   a. Republican presidential candidate Pat Robertson said he had some information about Soviet missiles hidden in Cuban caves and pointed out that "nobody can say for certain that those missiles aren't there."

   b. The Supreme Court ruled that no matter how upset it made Jerry Falwell, Larry Flynt had the right to make fun of him by claiming that he'd lost his virginity to his mother in an outhouse.

   c. Both of the above, plus Swaggart's own, ahem, peccadilloes were exposed—leading to a histrionic apology replete with gasps and sobs and an iconic faceful of flowing tears, though lacking any acknowledgment of the specificity of the sin—after Marvin Gorman scoresettlingly hired a photographer to take pictures of his enemy entering a motel room on Baton Rouge's Airline Highway with a prostitute named Debra Jo Murphree.

17. What did Jimmy Swaggart use to "disguise" himself when he frequented seedy motels with prostitutes?

    a. Varying combinations of hats, sunglasses, headbands, and combed-forward hair.

    b. Fake tattoos, though one clerk noted that "that boy wasn't foolin' nobody. Shit, he had ink on different arms at different times."

    c. Drag.

18. True or false? In her obligatory follow-up *Penthouse* nude spread, Deborah Jo Murphree said that she and Jimmy Swaggart had engaged in group sex.

    a. True. As she put it, "Threesomes, foursomes, and even moresomes."

    b. False. It turned out that Swaggart's thing was not sex but pornography—why, the very thing he'd been railing against as the scourge of humanity for his entire career!—and he basically told her to do a bunch of stuff that he masturbated to.

19. True or false? Though Jimmy Swaggart was initially suspended from broadcasting for three months, he wound up staying off the air for closer to a year.

    a. True. He took an honest look at himself and saw that he needed more time to mend.

    b. False. Though he was initially suspended for three months, he actually went back on the air far sooner, claiming, "If I do not return to the pulpit this weekend, millions of people will go to hell." This led his denomination to defrock him.

20. Why was Jimmy Swaggart driving on the wrong side of the road in October 1991 when he was stopped by police in Indio, California?

a. The desert heat made him a bit light-headed and he didn't realize he'd drifted over.

b. He didn't realize he was driving on a two-way road.

c. That was the side of the road that Rosemary Garcia, the prostitute he wanted to proposition, was standing on.

21. How did Rosemary Garcia explain being with Jimmy Swaggart?

a. "He's a man of God, and I need God's help, big time."

b. "He asked me for sex. I mean, that's why he stopped me. That's what I do. I'm a prostitute."

c. "He's just a delightful, *delightful* man."

22. True or false? Jimmy Swaggart's public groveling after his 1991 arrest convinced many that this time he'd finally seen the error of his ways.

a. True. There were no tears this time, but his contrition seemed all the more sincere for their absence.

b. False. This time there was no public apology. This time the line was, "The Lord told me it's flat none of your business."

23. Which tabloid broke the story in January 2001 that Reverend **JESSE JACKSON** had a twenty-month-old illegitimate daughter?

a. *National Enquirer.*

b. *Globe.*

c. *New York Post.*

24. When his top aide, Karin Stanford, was pregnant with his love child, where did Jesse Jackson take her?

   a. To Paris.

   b. To Rome.

   c. To the White House to meet and pose for photos with President Clinton, whom Jackson was counseling about repairing his marriage in the wake of the Monica Lewinsky scandal.

25. What precaution did Karin Stanford take in connection with the paternity of her child with Jesse Jackson?

   a. She kept a detailed log of when she and Jackson had sex.

   b. She entered his name as the baby's father on the birth certificate.

   c. She saved one of Jackson's used condoms, stored it in a freezer, then took it to a lab and established the DNA match.

With the Mark Foley scandal fresh in people's minds on the last weekend before the 2006 elections, **TED HAGGARD**, *president of the National Association of Evangelicals and "Pastor Ted" to the congregants of the New Life Church that he founded, made some unwelcome news.*

26. What was Ted Haggard's initial reaction to male prostitute/masseur Mike Jones's claims of having had crystal meth–fueled gay sex with him?

   a. "I'm steady with my wife."

   b. "I'm faithful to my wife."

   c. Both of the above, prefaced by, "I've never had a gay relationship with anybody."

27. According to his interview with the *Rocky Mountain News*, how did Mike Jones find out that the crystal meth–loving trick he knew as "Art"—Ted Haggard's middle name is Arthur— was actually the loudly profamily author of *From This Day Forward: Making Your Vows Last a Lifetime*?

   a. "I overheard him on his cell phone while I was in the bathroom and he was leaving someone a message and he said his name and left a phone number, and I remember thinking, 'Hagrid,' like in Harry Potter, but it wasn't, it was 'Haggard.'"

   b. "Someone gave me one of his books and I recognized the author photo."

   c. "*The Da Vinci Code* was out, and the History Channel was showing all these shows about it. There was one show about the Antichrist, and he appeared as an expert. It flashed his name for a moment. I didn't catch it, but I knew right away it was him. I thought, 'Oh my God, there he is. Oh my God, that's Art.' I think I was meant to know who he was because the next day I was at the gym working out about 5 A.M. Someone had put one of the TVs on Daystar, that Christian station. There he was again. I came home and went on the Internet and found out how huge he was. I thought to myself, 'Wow, this guy's big time.'"

28. According to Mike Jones, what did Ted Haggard say he liked to do before having sex with his wife?

   a. Have a massage.

   b. Pray.

   c. Snort crystal meth.

29. What made Mike Jones decide to expose "Art"?

  a. He was annoyed by Haggard calling him all the time wanting to buy crystal meth.

  b. He saw it as a viable way to impact the political process.

  c. He was offended by Haggard's hypocritical support for an amendment that would ban gay marriage in Colorado. "My favorite line that I hear, whether it's from George Bush or from Jerry Falwell or whoever, is they want to protect the sanctity of marriage. When I hear people say that, I get so infuriated because the same people that are saying that are probably the same people I'm sleeping with."

30. Where did Ted Haggard hold the media interview in which he told reporters that yeah, he did get a massage from Mike Jones but there was no sex involved, and as for the crystal meth, well, "I did call him. I called him to buy some meth, but I threw it away. . . . I never kept it very long because it was wrong. I was tempted. I bought it. But I never used it"?

  a. At a hastily arranged press conference in his Colorado Springs headquarters.

  b. At the local Applebee's.

  c. While he sat in his Chevy pickup with his wife and three young children in the truck.

31. Which of these voice-mail messages did Ted Haggard leave for Mike Jones?

    a. "Hi, Mike, this is Art. Hey, I was just calling to see if we could get any more. Either $100 or $200 supply. And I could pick it up really anytime. I could get it tomorrow or we could wait till next week sometime, and so I also wanted to get your address. I could send you some money for inventory, but that's probably not working, so if you have it, then go ahead and get what you can and I may buzz up there later today, but I doubt your schedule would allow that unless you have some in the house. Okay, I'll check in with you later. Thanks a lot, 'bye."

    b. "Hi, Mike, this is Art. I am here in Denver and sorry that I missed you. But as I said, if you want to go ahead and get the stuff, then that would be great. And I'll get it sometime next week or the week after or whenever. I will call you though early next week to, uh, see what's most convenient for you. Okay? Thanks a lot, 'bye."

    c. Both of the above, but wait, let's take a moment to imagine the mood in that Chevy as Haggard and his family drove away from the media.

32. In the face of the scandal, Ted Haggard was removed from the leadership of the National Association of Evangelicals. What happened a few months later?

    a. He announced that he'd made peace with his homosexuality and was beginning a gay-based ministry.

    b. He rejoined the community as if nothing had ever happened.

    c. After undergoing three weeks of counseling, he announced that he was "completely heterosexual" and that silly flying with Mike Jones was just some weird thing that happened once or twice or twenty or thirty or however many times during their three years of monthly get-togethers but never with anyone else like any of the many other men who came forward and claimed to have had sex with him, and certainly never again.

33. What other self-proclaimed nongay politician did Mike Jones say he had sex with?

   a. Jim West.

   b. Robert Bauman.

   c. Larry Craig.

34. True or false? According to a 2005 *Harper's* magazine profile, Ted Haggard spoke directly to George W. Bush or his advisers once a month.

   a. True. Bush's nickname for him was "Haggy."

   b. False. He spoke to the White House on a *weekly* basis.

Who said what?

35. "I sorrowfully acknowledge that seven years ago, in an isolated incident, I was wickedly manipulated by treacherous former friends and then colleagues who victimized me with the aid of a female confederate. They conspired to betray me into a sexual encounter at a time of great stress in my marital life."

   a. Jimmy Swaggart.

36. "I have sinned against you, my Lord, and I would ask that your precious blood would wash and cleanse every stain until it is in the seas of God's forgetfulness, never to be remembered again."

   b. Ted Haggard.

37. "The fact is I am guilty of sexual im- **c.** Jim Bakker.
morality. And I take responsibility for
the entire problem. I am a deceiver and
a liar. There's a part of my life that is so
repulsive and dark that I have been
warring against it for all of my adult
life."

38. On which Web site did Ted Haggard initially hook up with
Mike Jones?
   a. rentboy.com.
   b. hardboy.com.
   c. coxucker.com.
   d. craigsfist.com.

★ ★ ★ ★ ★

ANSWERS: 1. *a*, 2. *b*, 3. *b*, 4. *c*, 5. *c*, 6. *c*, 7. *d*, 8. *b*, 9. *b*, 10. *b*, 11.
a, 12. *a*, 13. *c*, 14. *a*, 15. *b*, 16. *c*, 17. *a*, 18. *b*, 19. *b*, 20. *c*, 21. *b*, 22.
b, 23. *a*, 24. *c*, 25. *c*, 26. *c*, 27. *c*, 28. *c*, 29. *c*, 30. *c*, 31. *c*, 32. *c*, 33.
c, 34. *b*, 35. *c*, 36. *a*, 37. *b*, 38. *a*.

LOCAL HEROES (#3)

ALFRED BLOOMINGDALE *was the husband of Betsy Bloom-ingdale, the best friend of First Lady Nancy Reagan, whose husband, Ronnie, doubtlessly at Nancy's insistence, appointed him to various advisory positions in his administration. His life ended in tabloid hell, Reagan's in dementia.*

1. How old was Vicki Morgan when fifty-four-year-old Alfred Bloomingdale met her in August 1969, right around the time of the Manson murders?

    a. Seventeen.

    b. Nineteen.

    c. Twelve.

2. For twelve years, Vicki Morgan was Alfred Bloomingdale's extremely well-kept mistress. What happened in 1982?

    a. Alfred Bloomingdale died of throat cancer.

    b. Vicki Morgan offered to keep quiet about Alfred's, er, esoteric sexual practices in exchange for sufficient funds to maintain her lavish lifestyle.

    c. Betsy Bloomingdale cut off every penny of the $18,000 a month that was being paid to Vicki Morgan.

    d. All of the above, plus Vicki Morgan sued the Bloomingdale estate for palimony.

3. True or false? Despite Betsy Bloomingdale's "Fuck you," Vicki Morgan kept secret the details of Alfred's sex life.

    a. True. It turned out that her love for him was too strong for her to betray him.

    b. False. "He was a Jekyll and Hyde," she said in a sworn deposition of his sexual proclivities. "Alfred was strange. I don't mean a fantasy. I mean a sickness. I truly mean a sickness." She said his eyes would glaze over and he would drool as he regularly bound women and beat them with his belt and sat on their backs as they crawled on the floor and did stuff with dildos and then finally would be aroused enough to fuck Morgan. "Alfred had a look in his eyes," she said of those bouts of lovemaking, "believe me when I say this, a look in his eyes and his face that scared me to death."

4. What did Alfred Bloomingdale say to Vicki Morgan after the first time they had the sex he was only able to have by inflicting horrific pain on women?

    a. "I assume you know this is not something to discuss with your friends."

    b. "I fucking hate myself when I do things like that."

    c. "Wasn't that fun?"

5. Complete Vicki Morgan's explanation of why she stayed with Alfred Bloomingdale despite what she referred to as "his Marquis de Sade complex": "Alfred is the most fascinating man I had ever met in my entire life. There is no one like him in the world. . . . He's _____"

    a. intense.

    b. a genius.

    c. childlike.

6. What was Vicki Morgan's plan to support herself after her palimony lawsuit was dismissed?

    a. Go back to school and become a sex therapist.

    b. Sell drugs.

    c. Write a tell-all book that would name all the wealthy and powerful men she'd been involved with, and then turn it into a miniseries, since wealthy and powerful men would obviously have no other recourse than to sit back helplessly and await their humiliation.

7. What happened not long after Vicki Morgan announced her intention to write her memoir?

    a. Her lawyer, Marvin Mitchelson of Lee Marvin pali-mony fame, said there was "definite interest . . . People are beating a path to her door."

    b. Marvin Mitchelson said there was also "lots of interest" in a TV miniseries based on the book.

    c. Marvin Mitchelson implied that the Reagans might turn up in the book and miniseries, since it was, after all, Nancy who'd first spotted Alfred and Vicki dining together and had informed Betsy.

    d. All of the above, and then, as if God were smiling on all those wealthy and powerful men she'd been plan-ning to expose, Marvin Pancoast—a gay friend she was renting a room to in the San Fernando Valley condo she was reduced to living in—beat her to death in her sleep.

8. What did Marvin Pancoast use to beat Vicki Morgan to death?

    a. One of Alfred's spiked belts that she'd kept as a souve-nir.

    b. A baseball bat.

    c. A dildo.

9. What was Marvin Pancoast's explanation for why he killed Vicki Morgan?

    a. "Vicki this, Vicki this, Vicki this, Vicki this—I just couldn't take it anymore."

    b. "She snored so loud I hadn't slept in days, and I just snapped."

    c. "Ed Meese paid me a lot of money to do it."

Who's who in the life of Mayor **ANTONIO VILLARAIGOSA** *(D-Los Angeles)?*

10. Kelly McBride. **a.** The woman Tony Villar married twenty years earlier whom he cheated on once before (while she was battling cancer!), whose name he grafted onto his own—*voilà!* Antonio Villaraigosa!—and whose name he held onto even after their divorce. How weird must that be for her?

11. Mirthala Salinas. **b.** The neighbor of Los Angeles mayor Antonio Villaraigosa's mistress who knew about the affair before anyone else because she came home one night and saw him in the lobby waiting for the elevator with bags of take-out food and a bottle of wine, and he introduced himself as Antonio and she said, "I know who you are. I know who you're going to see. Tell her I say hi," and the reason she was so sure was that everyone else in the complex was "older and Jewish" and "I knew he was not going to visit an elderly Jewish woman with wine and food."

12. Corina Raigosa. **c.** The Telemundo reporter who told viewers that "the rumors were true" about first-term Los Angeles mayor Antonio Villaraigosa's 2007 breakup with his wife without mentioning that she, as the mayor's mistress, was intimately involved in that split.

13. Jean Rouda.

d. The official at the Poynter Institute for Media Studies who said of the compromised reporter, "There really is no question that this is unacceptable. You can't sleep with your sources. This one sort of transcends the boundaries in any ethical newsroom."

The rumors of drug use and womanizing that plagued the career of **MARION BARRY** *throughout his first three terms as D.C. mayor dramatically shifted into the realm of fact one night in January 1990.*

Who's who?

14. Karen Johnson.

a. The longtime sex-and-drugs partner who cooperated with the sting and lured Marion Barry to a Vista International Hotel room and provided the crack he bought and smoked because she was pissed off that, at the height of her relationship with him several years earlier, he'd also been sleeping with some of her friends.

15. Linda Creque Maynard.

b. The Virgin Islands woman who testified that Marion Barry forced her into sex at a St. Thomas beachfront hotel.

16. Hazel Diane "Rasheeda" Moore.

c. The convicted crack dealer/former extramarital girlfriend of Marion Barry who described him as "very verbal in bed."

17. Bella Stumbo.   **d.** The old friend from the civil rights movement with whom Marion Barry did cocaine at the Mayflower Hotel in 1989.

18. Doris Crenshaw.   **e.** The *Los Angeles Times* reporter whose profile of Marion Barry—which included him saying, "I know that you can't be a good mayor high on drugs and alcohol," and "I'm going to continue to fight for a drug-free D.C.," and "Co-caaaaine? How folks use that stuff, anyhow? You put it up your *nooose?* No! Ooooooeeeeeee!" and "All this slander, about me chasing women—I'm innocent," and "I'm not stupid enough to have done the things they accuse me of! God gave me a good brain. What I have done nobody knows about because I don't get caught"—was published two weeks before an FBI sting videotaped him smoking crack in a hotel room with a longtime sex-and-drugs partner.

19. False or true? After the FBI burst into the room and told him he was under arrest, Marion Barry repeatedly referred to his temptress, Ms. Moore, as a "bitch."

  a. False. His arrest was so unexpected that he passed the next several minutes in stunned silence.

  b. True. "Bitch set me up," he said, "she set me up, I'll be goddamn . . . that bitch, that bitch did that to me. That bitch did that to me. Goddamn. Son of a bitch. She kept, kept, kept pushing me. Goddamn bitch . . . bitch kept insisting coming up here. Goddamn it, I should have known better. I should have known better."

20. What did Marion Barry say after returning from rehab but before being convicted of cocaine possession and serving six months in jail (for the 1989 Mayflower Hotel incident—the jury hung on all charges related to the 1990 Vista International Hotel sting)?

    a. With great indignance he complained that the devils in the sting operation made him do it: "They had me ingest cocaine, crack cocaine, which could have killed me. I could have been dead now with 70, 80, 90 percent pure cocaine."

    b. He said, "Even my most serious, most vociferous critics can't say the mayor is out making money selling drugs. . . . They can't say we shot anybody, we robbed anybody, that we had a scheme to steal a million dollars from the D.C. government," weirdly attempting to use his rectitude in not having done a bunch of things no one was accusing him of doing as a defense against having been caught on tape doing the thing he actually was accused of.

    c. He said the whole thing really wasn't that big a deal because "what's the worst [witnesses] could say, that I used cocaine with them? I think if you talked to most Washingtonians—even my supporters have some inklings that they may think I may have done that . . . So if they testify I'd used cocaine with them before, that's not damaging. People already think that. A lot of people do."

    d. He acknowledged, "I may be a poor role model," but added, "being a poor role model is not a crime."

    e. All of the above, plus he explained that the whole brouhaha was the result of his excessive altruism: "I spent so much time caring about and worrying about and doing for others, I've not worried about or cared enough for myself."

21. "You couldn't miss it. It was blatant. Right in front of every-body." What was prisoner Floyd Robertson talking about?

    a. Marion Barry in prison puffing on a crack pipe.

    b. Marion Barry in prison drinking from a pocket flask.

    c. Marion Barry getting a prison blow job from a female visitor.

22. When he said, "Those who do good sometimes suffer the most," who was Marion Barry comparing himself to?

    a. Martin Luther King Jr.

    b. Nelson Mandela.

    c. Jesus Christ and, for good measure, Mahatma Gandhi.

23. What was Marion Barry's slogan for his winning 1992 campaign for a seat on the city council?

    a. "Yesterday the Mayoralty, Today the City Council, To-morrow Who Knows? Maybe the Mayoralty Again."

    b. "He May Not Be Perfect, but He's Perfect for D.C."

    c. "He's Just Like Jesus, If Jesus Loved Cocaine."

24. True or false? After winning a fourth (nonconsecutive) term as mayor in 1994 and not running for reelection in 1998, Marion Barry began a run for a fifth term in 2002 but changed his mind after a mandatory drug test—the result of a guilty plea in connection with IRS-related misdemeanors—came back positive for cocaine and marijuana.

    a. True, and then it was back to rehab.

    b. False. He abandoned his mayoral race in 2002 after police found traces of cocaine and marijuana in his car. The mandatory drug test fiasco occurred three years later.

25. *The spirit of Marion Barry lives on in former Detroit mayor* **KWAME KILPATRICK**, *who took the oath of office in January 2002 and resigned in serious disgrace in September 2008. What honor did* Time *bestow on Kwame Kilpatrick in April 2005?*

　　a. He was named one of the 100 Most Influential Americans under Forty.

　　b. He was named one of the ten heaviest local officials.

　　c. He was named one of America's three worst big-city mayors.

Who's who in the life of Kwame Kilpatrick?

26. Christine Beatty.　**a.** The stripper who allegedly performed at a secret party in the fall of 2002 at the mayor's residence, the liltingly named Manoogian Mansion, and who was spotted by the mayor's wife while touching the mayor inappropriately when she came home unexpectedly, and who was then attacked with a wooden object by the mayor's wife, and who several months later died of multiple gunshot wounds sustained while sitting in her car—an act widely believed to have been a police department hit to cover up that party.

27. Tamara Greene.　**b.** The former high school sweetheart the mayor hired as his chief of staff and commenced to have a torrid affair with.

28. Carmen Slowski.　**c.** The woman—or a pseudonym for her—who stayed at a North Carolina hotel with him.

29. Mandi Wright. **d.** The photographer who was injured when Kilpatrick gestured angrily in reaction to a question about his latest extramarital conquest and struck her camera, shoving it into her face.

30. What did Christine Beatty say to the two cops who pulled her over in 2004 for speeding?
  a. "Do you know who the fuck I am?"
  b. "Sorry, sorry, sorry, sorry, sorry, really, I'm so so so so so sorry."
  c. "I'd let me slide if I were you. You see, I'm fucking the mayor."

31. What did Kwame Kilpatrick's father apologize for in 2005?
  a. Comparing news stories about his son's behavior to the "big lie" told by the Nazis to set up the Holocaust.
  b. Backing his vehicle into a TV camera van.
  c. Impregnating his mother with Kwame.

32. False or true? Kwame Kilpatrick and Christine Beatty initially denied their affair under oath.
  a. False. Both knew themselves to be too honest to fool anyone with a lie.
  b. True. Kilpatrick really gilded the lily, getting all huffy about how unfair these rumors were to his oh-oh so professional colleague: "My mother is a congresswoman. There have always been strong women around me. My aunt is a state legislator. I think it's absurd to assert that every woman that works with a man is a whore. I think it's disrespectful not just to Christine Beatty but to women who do a professional job that they do every single day. And it's also disrespectful to their families as well."

33. What made Kwame Kilpatrick and Christine Beatty stop their years of denying that they were having an affair?

    a. Someone got footage of them canoodling together in a restaurant on his cell phone.

    b. A motel room receipt turned up.

    c. The *Detroit Free Press* discovered some fourteen thousand text messages between them, and with Beatty messages such as "I really wanted to give you some good head this morning," and "I was about to jump your bones in Ford Field!" and "Then . . . while you're still deep inside of me . . . I would then ask you to gently grab my ass and you would put your finger in," and Kilpatrick messages such as "I'M ABOUT TO COME RIGHT NOW!" well, continued denial became not merely pointless but absurd.

Match the numbers that resolve the Kwame Kilpatrick scandal.

34. Four.

    a. Charges of obstruction of justice pled guilty to.

35. One.

    b. Charges of assaulting a police officer pled no contest to.

36. Two.

    c. Months of jail time sentenced to.

37. Five.

    d. Years of probation sentenced to, during which time public office cannot be held.

Who's who?

38. Brian White.

a. The reporter who discovered in 2005 that Kwame Kilpatrick arranged for a one-year lease for a luxury SUV to be used by his family by leasing it for $24,995—by happy coincidence, a mere $5 less than would have required approval by the city council.

39. Steve Wilson.

b. The sheriff's deputy whom Kwame Kilpatrick shoved.

40. Kenneth Cockrel Jr.

c. The city council president who became mayor of Detroit when Kwame Kilpatrick resigned in September 2008.

★ ★ ★ ★ ★

ANSWERS: 1. *a*, 2. *d*, 3. *b*, 4. *c*, 5. *c*, 6. *c*, 7. *d*, 8. *b*, 9. *a*, 10. *d*, 11. *c*, 12. *a*, 13. *b*, 14. *c*, 15. *b*, 16. *a*, 17. *e*, 18. *d*, 19. *b*, 20. *e*, 21. *c*, 22. *c*, 23. *b*, 24. *b*, 25. *c*, 26. *b*, 27. *a*, 28. *c*, 29. *d*, 30. *a*, 31. *a*, 32. *b*, 33. *c*, 34. *c*, 35. *b*, 36. *a*, 37. *d*, 38. *b*, 39. *a*, 40. *c*.

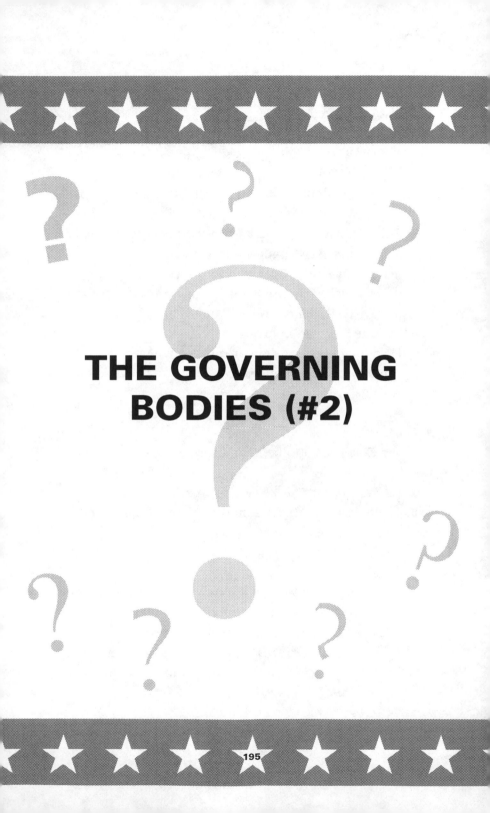

THE GOVERNING
BODIES (#2)

1. What prompted first-term New Jersey governor **JIM McGREEVEY**, in August 2004, to emerge from the closet with his wife, Dina, grimacing at his side, announce, "My truth is that I am a gay American," and resign?

    a. A photograph of him at a particularly raunchy gay bar began circulating on the Internet.

    b. A former gay lover he'd had on the state payroll—who later would insist none too convincingly that he was neither gay nor McGreevey's lover—was threatening to file a sexual harassment suit against him just in time for his reelection campaign unless he received millions of dollars to keep quiet.

    c. He'd found that he didn't really enjoy being governor and thought this would be a surefire way to get out of it.

2. What was notable about Jim McGreevey's appointment of his lover Golan Cipel to be New Jersey's first homeland security chief?

    a. No background check was run on him.

    b. There was no official announcement of the appointment to the newly created position.

    c. As a foreign national (from Israel), Cipel didn't qualify for a federal security clearance.

    d. All of the above, plus—despite inflated claims to the contrary—Cipel had zero experience in the fields of security and counterterrorism he was now to oversee. And this was terrorism we were dealing with, not shoplifting. Again, for the record, zero experience, but give him the job anyway, what the hell.

3. False or true? After six months of escalating controversy about Golan Cipel's appointment, Jim McGreevey accepted his resignation as homeland security chief but gave him a new job as his special "policy counselor."

    a. False. He wisely took the opportunity to cut his losses and severed all official ties with him.

    b. True. He even continued to pay him his $110,000 salary.

4. Why did Golan Cipel finally leave the employ of the State of New Jersey?

    a. An investigation by Gannett New Jersey found that "McGreevey relied on exaggerated anti-terrorism credentials to justify" hiring him.

    b. He got a better offer from the State of New York.

    c. His work visa ran out.

5. Golan Cipel came to the United States with a work visa sponsored by major McGreevey contributor Charles Kushner. What story about Kushner broke a month before Jim McGreevey's surprise resignation?

    a. He was an Israeli in the United States under false pretenses.

    b. He was under consideration for a job in a Kerry administration.

    c. He was under federal investigation for tax fraud and illegal campaign contributions, so he embarked on a blackmail scheme in which he paid a prostitute $10,000 to have secretly taped sex with a key witness against him (his brother-in-law), then sent the video to the man's wife (his own sister!).

6. True or false? Jim McGreevey was having a brilliant first term and was coasting to reelection when he was brought down by his homosexuality.

    a. True. There was even some talk of his seeking the presidency in 2008.

    b. False. His popularity was less than 40 percent, two of his close associates were dogged by scandal, and mere weeks before news of his homosexuality broke, there was open talk among New Jersey Democrats about the possibility of replacing McGreevey with another candidate.

7. What else did the public learn in 2007 and 2008 during the increasingly unpleasant eighteen-months-long divorce proceedings between Jim and Dina McGreevey?

    a. Dina didn't like the idea of their five-year-old daughter sleeping in the same bed with her father and his lover, Mark O'Donnell (an Australian money manager, not the brilliant New York playwright), under a life-size photograph of a nude male model (though Jim pointed out that the girl didn't actually sleep there but merely came in when she felt ill or insecure, and that the offending portrait had been removed).

    b. Dina's insistence on the cancellation of a birthday party Jim was planning for their daughter because it wasn't his weekend to have her prompted the judge in the case to observe, "The hatred that these two have for each other overrides everything, including their child."

    c. Both of the above, plus his former chauffeur Teddy Pedersen came forward with the news—confirmed by McGreevey—that he, McGreevey, and Dina used to have three-way sex. "We called it the Friday Night Special," he said. "I was always with them. We traveled together, went on vacations, shared the same room."

8. Which of these was number one on David Letterman's top ten list of chapter titles in Jim McGreevey's memoir *The Confession*?

   a. "At First I Just Thought I Was Bipartisan."

   b. "How to Pretend to Like Girls for 47 Years."

   c. "Politicians Who Left a Bad Taste in My Mouth."

   d. "Why I Don't Like Bush."

9. How did hooker Ashley Dupre find out that the guy she had sex with on February 13, 2008, at Washington's Mayflower Hotel was New York governor **ELIOT SPITZER**?

   a. The booker at her escort service told her who she was going to see, and to be "extra nice to him."

   b. She had seen him on *The Colbert Report* the night before their encounter.

   c. Her mother called and told her to turn on the TV to see him resigning. "I was there for a purpose—not to wonder who [he] could be," she explained her ignorance to *People*. "I was wrapped up in my family, my music. I knew the name, but the face . . . I'm not really a TV person."

10. How was Eliot Spitzer known to the Emperors Club VIP escort service?

   a. "Client 9."

   b. "High Black Socks."

   c. "The Guv'nor."

11. What aliases were Eliot Spitzer and Ashley Dupre using for their rendezvous?

   a. He was "George Fox" and she was "Kristen."

   b. He was "John Doe" and she was "Tiffany."

   c. He was "Eliot Ness" and she was "Monique."

12. How did Eliot Spitzer get caught?

a. His good friend whose name he was using as an alias found out, got pissed off, and called the police.

b. He was caught on a wiretap during an investigation that was started because of his suspicious shifting of money from one account to another to avoid it being identified as payment for hookers.

c. Ashley Dupre was so excited to have serviced the governor of New York that she e-mailed several friends about it, and those e-mails wound up on the Smoking Gun Web site.

13. How did Ashley Dupre describe their encounter?

a. "He was really friendly, really interested in me, in my job. He said I reminded him of someone he went to school with."

b. "He kept referring to himself as a 'fucking steam-roller,' which I found a little disconcerting."

c. "Some guys, they want to have conversation and really get to know each other. With him, it clearly was not like that. It was more of a transaction. Strictly business."

14. True or false? Ashley Dupre's father stopped speaking to her after the Spitzer story broke.

a. True. He told her she had "humiliated" him.

b. False. He called her up and said with some pride, "Damn, girl. When you do it, you do it big."

15. True or false? Eliot Spitzer was a favorite among the girls at the Emperors Club VIP escort service.

    a. True. He had a reputation as a big tipper and a "fun guy."

    b. False. He had a reputation for being "difficult" because, as the booker told Ashley Dupre, he sometimes asked his hookers "to do things that, like, you might not think were safe."

16. How much did Eliot Spitzer pay for the tryst that brought him down?

    a. $1,500.

    b. $2,500.

    c. $4,300, but part of that was a down payment on a next time that never came.

17. What was the impact of a bill Eliot Spitzer signed into law soon after taking office as governor of New York?

    a. It decriminalized medical marijuana.

    b. It tripled the fine for smoking in public buildings.

    c. It increased the penalties for patronizing prostitutes, quadrupling the three-month maximum jail term to a year.

18. What did Ashley Dupre say she didn't want to be thought of by the public as?

    a. "A monster."

    b. "Pathetic."

    c. "Slutty."

19. Who wrote a *New York Times* op-ed piece in the wake of the Spitzer scandal in which she decried the pressure on the innocent wife to be seen lending grim-faced support to the humiliated spouse as he publicly acknowledges his stupidity and his sins?

    a. Dina Matos McGreevey.

    b. Lee Hart.

    c. Elizabeth Edwards.

    d. Wendy Vitter.

Who wrote what?

20. Roger Simon in Politico.

    a. "If stupidity ever gets to $200 a barrel, I want drilling rights to Eliot Spitzer's head."

21. Gail Collins in the *New York Times*.

    b. "Memo to future disgraced politicians: The nation has discussed this at length, and we do not want to see any more stricken spouses at the press conference."

22. Ashley Dupre on her MySpace page.

    c. "I am all about my music, and my music is all about me."

23. What did **DAVID PATERSON** reveal as he took office replacing Eliot Spitzer as governor of New York?

    a. That he would consider naming himself to Hillary Clinton's Senate seat if she was elected president.

    b. That he wouldn't consider naming himself to Hillary Clinton's Senate seat if she was elected president.

    c. That several years earlier, in response to an affair of his wife, Michelle, he'd had affairs with "a number of women," though he took pains to be clear that although he was "jealous over Michelle," his serial philandering was "not her fault."

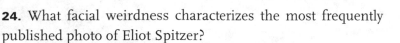

24. What facial weirdness characterizes the most frequently published photo of Eliot Spitzer?

  a. His eyes are crossed.

  b. His nose is swollen.

  c. His lips are so tightly closed that they appear sewn shut.

ANSWERS: 1. *b*, 2. *d*, 3. *b*, 4. *a*, 5. *c*, 6. *b*, 7. *c*, 8. *d*, 9. *c*, 10. *a*, 11. *a*, 12. *b*, 13. *c*, 14. *b*, 15. *b*, 16. *c*, 17. *c*, 18. *a*, 19. *a*, 20. *a*, 21. *b*, 22. *c*, 23. *c*, 24. *c*.

THE GARYS

1. *Former Colorado senator* **GARY HART** *announced his entry into the 1988 presidential race with the prophetic statement "As a candidate I can almost guarantee that I'm going to make some mistakes." Rumors of womanizing had dogged his first run for the Democratic presidential nomination in 1984, and they were in the front of reporters' minds in April 1987.*

1. What did Hart tell E. J. Dionne on the subject for a profile that ran in the *New York Times Magazine* on May 3, 1987?
- **a.** "Isn't the Jim Bakker thing enough? How many sex scandals does the press need at any given moment?"
- **b.** "It depends what the meaning of 'womanizing' is."
- **c.** "Follow me around. I don't care. I'm serious. If anybody wants to put a tail on me, go ahead. They'd be very bored."

2. What other stories did people around the country wake up to on the Sunday morning that Gary Hart's challenge to the press appeared?
- **a.** "Killer crocodiles" were "on the rise" in northern Australia.
- **b.** President Reagan was calling for more money for the Nicaraguan rebels known as the "contras."
- **c.** The fiftieth anniversary of the *Hindenburg* zeppelin crash was still three days away.
- **d.** Lots of teams beat lots of other teams in baseball, basketball, and hockey games.
- **e.** All of the above, plus several reporters from the *Miami Herald* had already put a tail on Hart, and they'd been anything but bored, since they staked out his house and found that he'd spent Friday night and much of Saturday in his Washington, D.C., town house with twenty-nine-year-old actress/model Donna Rice.

3. Who is Bill Broadhurst?

   a. The former adviser to Gary Hart who said, "He's always in jeopardy of having the sex issue raised if he can't keep his pants on."

   b. The reporter to whom Gary Hart once burbled, "I love danger!"

   c. The former adviser to Gary Hart who had to remind him to kiss his wife after announcing his first race for the presidency.

   d. The friend of Gary Hart's whose house Hart claimed Donna Rice actually stayed at with Lynn Armandt, the friend of Rice's who'd flown up from Miami with her.

   e. The reporter who made Gary Hart the first presidential candidate to be asked directly by the press, "Have you ever committed adultery?"—a question he initially resisted but that finally elicited his acknowledgment that he hadn't been "absolutely and totally faithful to my wife."

   f. The press secretary who said Gary Hart was "offended and outraged. He's furious. He's a victim."

   g. The reporter who explained the press's obsession with Gary Hart's sex life by saying, "I don't have any reason to believe Michael Dukakis goes to Bimini on boats with blondes. Gary Hart is the sole point of interest on this because he was the one with the reputation."

   h. The columnist who wrote of Gary Hart's risk in bringing an attractive young woman to his home given his reputation, "His intentions are irrelevant. It's the stupidity of what he did that is devastating. . . . What is incomprehensible in a man with his resources is the lack of discretion and the humiliation he inflicted on his wife."

4. How did Gary Hart refer to Donna Rice?

    a. "The woman in question."

    b. "Someone Don Henley introduced me to."

    c. "That woman—Miss Rice."

5. Though claiming that he had "no personal relationship" with Donna Rice, Gary Hart acknowledged that he'd phoned her several times recently from the campaign trail. What did she say they talked about?

    a. "The Jim Bakker scandal."

    b. "How the press was beating on him."

    c. "Lots of things. You know, stuff. How weird Michael Jackson is getting."

6. What was the hilariously apropos name of the chartered yacht on which Gary Hart and Donna Rice and Lynn Armandt and Bill Broadhurst turned out to have taken an overnight cruise from Miami to Bimini?

    a. *Hanky-Panky.*

    b. *Monkey Business.*

    c. *Making Whoopee.*

7. How did Donna Rice's friend Lynn Armandt honor their friendship?

    a. She originally tipped off reporters that Rice was flying to Washington from Miami to spend the weekend with Gary Hart.

    b. After Rice claimed that she actually spent the weekend with Armandt at Bill Broadhurst's place, she said no, Rice actually spent the night with Hart.

c. After Rice claimed that the women and men spent the night of the cruise on separate boats, she said no, Rice spent the night with Hart.

d. All of the above, plus she sold the photo of Donna Rice in Gary Hart's lap—one of the most famous images in modern American politics—to the *National Enquirer*.

8. What was Gary Hart's explanation for that photo?

a. "People pose for pictures with candidates all the time. Sometimes they're even good-looking."

b. "The attractive lady whom I had only recently been introduced to dropped into my lap. I chose not to dump her off."

c. "You want the truth? I pulled her down on my lap to hide my erection."

9. Two of these quotes came from Gary Hart's wife, Lee. Which one came from Donna Rice?

a. "If it doesn't bother me, I don't think it ought to bother anyone else."

b. "If I could have been planning his weekend schedule, I think I would have scheduled it differently."

c. "Any stupid publisher who doesn't want [a book about my life] has his head up his butt."

10. Why did Gary Hart withdraw from the presidential race?

a. His family demanded it.

b. The *Washington Post* was about to break the story of one of his less ambiguous extramarital affairs.

c. He realized his sex life would be seriously curtailed if he kept campaigning.

11. False or true? Gary Hart's announcement of his withdrawal from the presidential race, in which he basically blamed the press for his getting caught with a woman not his wife, was reminiscent of Richard Nixon's famous drunken rant blaming the press for his loss of the 1962 California gubernatorial election.

- **a.** False. Nixon had been all stubbly and Hart was clean-shaven.
- **b.** True. There had always been something essentially Nixonesque about Hart—another resentful son of an emotionally austere mother, always hypersensitive to slights real or imagined—and his press conference was so Nixonian that Nixon himself wrote Hart a letter congratulating him for "handling a very difficult situation uncommonly well."

When a twenty-four-year-old intern went missing in Washington, D.C., in May 2001—her body was found in Rock Creek Park a year later—the big rumor was that she'd been dating a congressman. But who? Enter **GARY CONDIT,** *a conservative Democratic representative from Modesto, California, and the married father of two, including a daughter older than the intern he was having an affair with.*

12. What made police suspect that the mystery man Chandra Levy was dating was a congressman?

- **a.** In an e-mail to a friend the previous Christmas, she'd written, "My man will be coming back here when Congress starts up again. I'm looking forward to seeing him."
- **b.** They found notebooks on which she'd written over and over, "Mrs. Congressman."
- **c.** Her car sported the bumper sticker CONGRESSMEN KNOW HOW TO SCREW YOU.

13. By what nickname was Gary Condit known to his constituents?

   a. "Mr. Blow Dry."

   b. "Ken Doll."

   c. "The Lizard King."

14. False or true? Gary Condit's PR team pronounced that his third interview with police—the one in which he finally admitted having an affair with Chandra Levy—"was a home run."

   a. False. What would that even mean, anyway?

   b. True. A "home run"? What the fuck did that mean?

15. What did Gary Condit do to make people of even modest intelligence think, "This scumbag is hiding something"?

   a. He admitted that Chandra Levy (whom he described as "a great person and a good friend") had visited his Washington apartment four or five times—his wife, Carolyn, lived back home in Modesto—but refused to elaborate on the relationship.

   b. Three weeks after admitting that Chandra Levy had visited his apartment, he admitted that she'd slept over but refused to elaborate on the sleeping arrangements.

   c. A month after admitting that Chandra Levy had slept at his apartment, he admitted that it had been with him.

   d. He lawyered up with Abbe Lowell, a heavyweight who defended President Clinton in the House impeachment hearings.

   e. He tried to get Anne Marie Smith, the United Airlines flight attendant he'd been having a year-long affair with, to sign an affidavit denying that they'd had an affair.

   f. All of the above and lots more, such as telling police he couldn't recall if he and Chandra Levy had sex the last time he saw her.

16. True or false? Though Gary Condit had spent the summer of 2001 developing a reputation as one of the slimiest politicians in America, he turned it all around by giving an unexpectedly soul-baring interview to Connie Chung.

    a. True. His popularity ratings more than doubled literally overnight.

    b. False. The sit-down with Connie Chung was an unimaginably self-destructive performance and an obvious career-ender for Condit, who still refused to bow out gracefully and so was defeated in the March 2002 primary.

17. What happened during the half hour that Gary Condit spent chatting with Connie Chung?

    a. He denied being a murderer. ("Did you kill Chandra Levy?" "I did not.")

    b. He denied having stonewalled the investigation and declared absurdly, "I don't think there's anyone in Washington, D.C., who's been more cooperative in this investigation than myself."

    c. He said he "never lied" to Chandra Levy's mother even though she says he told her he wasn't having an affair with her daughter, and said he was "sorry if she misunderstood the conversations."

    d. He explained that the reason he threw away the watch box from a gift given to him by an unnamed woman— and wait, not just tossed it out but took it to Virginia and discarded it there, which we know because he was spotted by a passerby with his arm deep inside an Alexandria trash can—was "because I was cleaning out my office, to be very frank with you" and had nothing to do with the fact that the police were coming to search his apartment.

e. Asked if he and Chandra Levy were "in love," he said, "I don't know that she was in love with me. She never said so," adding coldly, "and I was not in love with her."

f. He repeatedly observed—as if it wasn't patently obvious—that throughout his thirty-four-year marriage he hadn't been "a perfect man."

g. He said he couldn't answer specific questions about his sexual relationship with Chandra Levy "out of respect" for a "specific request from the Levy family," thus using the family's expression of revulsion at the very idea of those details as a shield to keep from revealing them.

h. He refused to answer all variations on the basic question "Did you sleep with her?"

i. All of the above, plus he referred to his wife as "that woman."

Match the results of an NBC News poll taken after Connie Chung's interview with Gary Condit.

18. 71 percent. **a.** Americans who were "very unsatisfied" with his explanation for not cooperating fully with the police.

19. 93 percent. **b.** Americans who believed there were things about which he knew more than he was telling.

20. 81 percent. **c.** Americans who thought he was less concerned about Levy's fate than he was about his political career.

21. 84 percent. **d.** Americans who wouldn't vote for him if he was their representative.

22. What does Gary Condit have in common with Lizzie Grubman and Mariah Carey?

- **a.** They're all Geminis.
- **b.** None of them is Jewish.
- **c.** They were all dealing with unfavorable publicity during the summer of 2001 and were all instantly forgotten by midmorning on September 11, 2001, prompting the *Onion* headline "A Shattered Nation Longs to Care about Stupid Bullshit Again."

ANSWERS: 1. *c*, 2. *e*, 3. *d*, 4. *a*, 5. *b*, 6. *b*, 7. *d*, 8. *b*, 9. *c*, 10. *b*, 11. *b*, 12. *a*, 13. *a*, 14. *b*, 15. *f*, 16. *b*, 17. *i*, 18. *b*, 19. *d*, 20. *c*, 21. *a*, 22. *c*.

THE IMPEACHERS

A funny thing happened to five of the people most publicly out-raged, offended, and incensed by the tawdry, sordid, immoral be-havior of President Bill Clinton.

BOB BARR *was an archconservative Republican congressman from the eastern suburbs of Atlanta, Georgia, who spent much of his energy during his four terms in office hounding the Clintons, ulti-mately coming into his own as one of the House managers during the 1998 impeachment hearings. He left the Republican Party in 2004 and was the Libertarian Party's 2008 presidential candidate, receiving 0.4 percent of the vote.*

1. Which of these descriptions of Bob Barr came from *Washington Post* writer Peter Carlson?
- **a.** "The idol of the gun-toting, abortion-fighting, IRS-hating hard right wing of American politics."
- **b.** "Mr. Conservative Prig."
- **c.** "Not a guy you'd want to be stuck in an elevator with, let alone a foxhole."
- **d.** "A thrice-married proponent of family values who once warned, during a speech attacking gay marriage, that the 'flames of hedonism, the flames of narcissism, the flames of self-centered morality are licking at the foundations of our society, the family unit.'"
- **e.** "The possessor of one of those mustaches that you'd like to see someone remove slowly with tweezers, whisker by whisker."

2. What was conservative prig Bob Barr seen licking off the chests of two big-breasted women at a 1992 Cobb County, Georgia, Leukemia Society fund-raiser?
- **a.** Whipped cream.
- **b.** Honey.
- **c.** Chocolate syrup.

3. True or false? The day after the Monica Lewinsky story broke, Bob Barr introduced a resolution directing the House Judiciary Committee to look into the possibility of instituting impeachment proceedings against Bill Clinton.

    a. True. Barr felt very strongly that moral transgressions were every bit as egregious as criminal ones.

    b. False. Barr hated Bill Clinton so much that he'd actually introduced that resolution months before anyone outside of her family and friends had ever heard the name Monica Lewinsky.

4. True or false? While Bob Barr was out there shrieking daily for the impeachment of Bill Clinton, *Hustler* publisher Larry Flynt's investigators revealed that Barr also had used a cigar for purposes unconnected with inhaling tobacco smoke.

    a. True. Barr threatened a lawsuit and the charge was retracted.

    b. False. What they found, according to his second wife, was that Barr—one of the most vociferous opponents of abortion—not only didn't object to his second wife's having one, but also drove her to and from the procedure, which he paid for—possibly because he was already having an affair with the woman who would become his third wife.

5. True or false? On *Da Ali G Show*, Bob Barr was one of the customers at the country and western bar happily singing along to Borat's "Throw the Jew down the Well."

    a. True. When confronted with the footage he claimed that he thought they were singing "Throw the *shoe* down the well."

    b. False. He did, however, appear in *Borat: Cultural Learnings of America for Make Benefit Glorious Nation of Kazakhstan,* in which he was given cheese described by Borat as having been made from his wife's breast milk.

6. Which of these statements is *not* true?

   a. The 2002 *Almanac of American Politics* described Bob Barr as "humorless, pessimistic, sarcastic, to the point that his wife beeps him when he is on TV, 'Smile, honey.'"

   b. Though Bob Barr authored the 1996 law prohibiting the federal government from recognizing same-sex marriages, as the 2008 Libertarian Party candidate, he was for recognizing those marriages.

   c. An Atlanta lawyer said of Bob Barr, "He's certainly not a hail-fellow-well-met. When he tells a funny story, you have to think twice about whether to laugh."

   d. Though Bob Barr used to be one of the most vociferous opponents of medical marijuana—saying of it in 2002, "This is not medicine. It is bogus witchcraft"—as the 2008 Libertarian Party candidate, he was for it.

   e. Bob Barr is a distant cousin of Roseanne Barr.

   f. Though Bob Barr voted for the Patriot Act and for the Iraq war, as the 2008 Libertarian Party candidate, he was against both of them.

HELEN CHENOWETH *was a three-term Republican representative from Idaho whose antipathy toward any type of government regulation probably contributed to her not wearing a seat belt on the day in October 2006 when she was thrown from her car and killed.*

7. What did Helen Chenoweth do mere days after Dan Burton announced that he'd fathered a child out of wedlock?

   a. She announced that she'd mothered a child out of wedlock.

   b. She admitted that, in the 1980s, she'd had a long affair with a married man.

   c. She held one of her "endangered salmon bake" fundraisers where canned salmon was served to mock the notion of Idaho salmon as an endangered species, which she felt it couldn't be since she was able to walk into a supermarket and buy some whenever she damn well pleased.

8. What did Helen Chenoweth say made her six-year affair with married man Vernon Ravenscroft less offensive than President Clinton's transgressions?
   a. It happened before she held public office.
   b. She was no longer married when she began the affair.
   c. Both of the above, plus at least she was virtuous enough to answer honestly when asked directly about it.

9. True or false? Helen Chenoweth had already admitted to this affair three years earlier, in a 1995 interview.
   a. True. The story ran during the O. J. Simpson trial, so it made no real splash and was quickly forgotten.
   b. False. When asked directly about the affair three years earlier, she'd said, "For heaven's sakes, that is low. That is so bizarre. I'm utterly speechless. My official answer would have to be, this indicates a measure of desperation. When they can't debate the issues, they turn to character assassination. . . . People who know me know better than that. People who know Mr. Ravenscroft's fine family know better." Wow, what an *honest* answer.

10. What did wronged wife Harriet Ravenscroft say about Helen Chenoweth's constant ranting about President Clinton's immorality?
   a. "The lady doth protest too much."
   b. "As you can imagine I'm not a fan, but I can't help agreeing with her on this matter."
   c. "I don't see how Helen can live with herself and do this."

11. What good news did Helen Chenoweth share about her long-ago affair?

   a. "I've asked for God's forgiveness, and I've received it."

   b. "We've managed to remain friends all these years."

   c. "Mr. Ravenscroft was quite the swordsman."

12. Complete a Republican operative's comment about Helen Chenoweth, as reported by *Salon* in 1998: "Helen is living proof that _____"

   a. good looks will get you pretty far.

   b. being a total nut is no bar to getting elected to Congress.

   c. you *can* fuck your brains out.

For a moment in the fall of 1998, it looked like Louisiana Republican **BOB LIVINGSTON** *was about to become Speaker of the House. Then the moment passed.*

13. How much time went by between Bob Livingston's securing enough votes to ensure his election as Speaker of the House and his sad announcement that, though he knew he'd do a good job, he had to decline the post after all?

   a. Two weeks.

   b. A month.

   c. Forty days.

14. False or true? Bob Livingston's surprise announcement that he'd strayed from his marriage was prompted by an overwhelming sense of guilt.

   a. False. He'd gotten wind that a story about his marital infidelities was about to run in *Hustler* magazine. As he told colleagues, "I've been Larry Flynt-ed."

   b. True. As he told colleagues, "You know, glass houses and all that. I feel bad about attacking Clinton for this when I did it, too."

15. True or false? After seeing his ad in the *Washington Post* offering money to anyone who could shed unwelcome light on the private lives of the moral scolds baying the loudest for impeachment, three women came forward to tell Larry Flynt's investigators that they'd had sex with Bob Livingston.

    a. True. Two of them used the phrase "lousy lay."

    b. False. It was four women.

16. Complete Bob Livingston's statement differentiating President Clinton's horrific-to-the-point-of-being-impeachable offenses from his own relatively minor ones: "I want to assure everyone that _____"

    a. [my] indiscretions were not with employees on my staff, and I have never been asked to testify under oath about them.

    b. no one's going to come out of my woodwork screaming rape.

    c. I don't even smoke cigars, let alone use them as sex toys.

17. True or false? When House Speaker-elect Bob Livingston read a statement confessing his past marital infidelities, his Republican colleagues sat in stunned silence, and some even started to boo him.

    a. True. More than a few of them grumbled that he should have mentioned something about it before running for Speaker.

    b. False. When Livingston said he'd cheated on his wife, what they actually did, as if the Congress had suddenly been transported to Superman's Bizarro World, was leap to their feet and give him a standing ovation. Honest.

18. False or true? Bob Livingston's House seat was filled by David Vitter, who went on to star in an even bigger sex scandal after being elected to the Senate.

  a. False. Vitter was already a member of Congress when Livingston resigned.

  b. True. A much bigger sex scandal that had the word "diapers" attached to it.

Representative **DAN BURTON** *(R-IN) has been in Congress since 1983, and apparently no amount of egregious behavior is too much for his constituents.*

19. True or false? Dan Burton, convinced that Clinton aide Vince Foster didn't commit suicide and that the president had him killed, reenacted the "murder" in his backyard.

  a. True. He fired a handgun into "a head-like thing" believed to have been a pumpkin.

  b. False. Why, that would make him a virtual madman.

20. How did Dan Burton explain his ardor for the impeachment of President Bill Clinton?

  a. "He literally got away with murder."

  b. "Something about him just rubs me the wrong way."

  c. "This guy's a scumbag, that's why I'm after him."

21. What prompted Harrison Ullmann, the editor of an alternative weekly in Indianapolis, to publish a column that called Dan Burton's own moral rectitude into question and opened the floodgates to further investigations?

  a. He was repelled by Burton calling President Clinton a "scumbag."

  b. He received a videotape of Burton cavorting with two hookers.

  c. He was stunned by the hypocrisy of Burton's campaign mantra, "Character *does* matter."

22. Fearful that his biggest secret was about to be published in *Vanity Fair,* what skeleton did Dan Burton bring out of his own closet and introduce to the nation even as he was shrieking for President Clinton's scalp?

    a. He flirted with liberalism in college.

    b. He once gave his wife an STD.

    c. He fathered a boy out of wedlock.

23. How old was Dan Burton's bastard son when his existence was revealed to the public?

    a. Three.

    b. Fifteen.

    c. Twenty-two.

24. In 1990, Dan Burton introduced a bill mandating the death penalty for drug dealers. What happened in 1994?

    a. The number of drug dealers in the United States hit its lowest level in two decades.

    b. Dan Burton accompanied a SWAT team on a drug raid.

    c. Dan Burton's nonbastard eighteen-year-old son Dan Burton Jr. was arrested in a car packed with almost eight pounds of marijuana that he and a friend were transporting across state lines from Louisiana to Indiana, and then, five months later, while still awaiting trial for that offense, he was rearrested when police found thirty marijuana plants and a shotgun in his apartment. Needless to say, not only wasn't he executed—that law, of course, never passed—but he served not one day in jail.

25. During a March 1995 hearing on the drug scourge, Dan Burton suggested that the U.S. military should place an aircraft carrier off the coast of which landlocked nation?

   a. Paraguay.

   b. Bolivia.

   c. Afghanistan.

26. What was Dan Burton referring to when he told his House colleagues, "I want to apologize to you if this matter has caused you any embarrassment"?

   a. His having called President Clinton a "scumbag."

   b. His turning out to have an illegitimate son.

   c. His release of selected portions of taped prison conversations between longtime Clinton friend Webster Hubbell and his wife that were edited—completely unintentionally, mind you—to omit all of the many exculpatory comments about the Clintons in connection with an investigation into their fund-raising for the 1996 campaign.

27. After House Speaker Newt Gingrich apologized for Dan Burton's edited tape stunt, Burton shot back that he wasn't embarrassed about it. What was Gingrich's reply?

   a. "You don't embarrass easy, do you?"

   b. "I know you meant well, but next time try not to be so cute."

   c. "Then I'm embarrassed for you, I'm embarrassed for myself, and I'm embarrassed for . . . the circus that went on at your committee."

28. In addition to the bastard thing, what other allegations of impropriety have been made against Dan Burton?

   a. He groped a lobbyist.

   b. He's had sex with many women who have worked for him.

c. He makes illegal telephone solicitations for money from federal premises (i.e., his office) and warns his would-be contributors, "If you know what's good for you, you'll get me my money."

d. He was known when he was in the Indiana legislature as "the biggest skirt-chaser" there.

e. All of the above, plus he was renowned not just for philandering but also for sexual harassment. As one female lobbyist said, "Everybody who was around him at the Statehouse and everyone who knows him at all says the same thing: God, how did Dan Burton get away with this?"

29. In January 2007 Dan Burton cast the only vote against a bill that _____

a. made gay-bashing a hate crime.

b. raised the minimum wage.

c. banned members of Congress from accepting gifts and free trips from lobbyists.

Illinois Republican **HENRY HYDE**—*who described the family as "the surest basis of civil order, the strongest foundation for free enterprise, the safest home of freedom"—was House manager of the 1998 impeachment hearings when it was revealed that his own record for moral rectitude was hardly unblemished.*

30. How old was Henry Hyde when he indulged himself in what he looked back on bemusedly as "youthful indiscretions"?

a. His early twenties.

b. His midthirties.

c. Pretty much his entire forties.

31. What did Henry Hyde's "youthful indiscretions" consist of?

    a. A brief flirtation with a lobbyist that was never consummated.

    b. A couple of one-night stands that were the results of too much drinking at parties.

    c. Among others, a seven-year affair with a married woman named Cherie Snodgrass, whom he "kept" in an apartment so they'd have a trysting place.

32. True or false? The fact that Henry Hyde was unmarried and childless at the time of the affair made the whole thing less unseemly than it would have been if, say, he'd been married and the father of four.

    a. True. Ironically, Hyde met the woman who would become his wife the night after ending the affair with Snodgrass.

    b. False. Had Hyde been unmarried and childless, yes, that would have decreased the sordidness a bit, but as it happens he was married and the father of four throughout the affair.

33. False or true? Cuckold Fred Snodgrass told *Salon* that after he discovered his wife's secret apartment, he went over there and wanted to confront her and Henry Hyde, but he couldn't get in because Hyde was keeping the door shut by leaning his considerable bulk against it.

    a. False. The last thing Snodgrass wanted was to make a scene.

    b. True. He told *Salon*, "Some guy is holding the door, pushing back. It was Hyde. And he's a big guy, I couldn't get in. My wife said she used to tell him, 'What are you doing, trying to hit three hundred?'"

34. What did Fred Snodgrass tell *Salon* about Henry Hyde during the Clinton impeachment drama?

   a. "I hate the man."

   b. "He had an affair with a young woman with three children. At least the president didn't do that."

   c. Both of the above, and also, "I watched him on TV the other night. These politicians were going on about how he should have been on the Supreme Court, what a great man he is, how we're lucky to have him in Congress in charge of the impeachment case. And all I can think of is here is this man, this hypocrite who broke up my family."

35. What did Cherie Snodgrass's daughter tell *Salon* about her mother?

   a. "She still talks about [Hyde] all the time. He was the love of her life."

   b. "She said despite it all she'd vote for [Hyde] if she lived in his district."

   c. "She's just so fed up with [Hyde], with how two-faced he is. She knows she wasn't his first [mistress] and she wasn't his last. She hates his anti-abortion stuff, and all the family-values stuff. She thinks he's bad for the country, he's too powerful and he's hypocritical."

★ ★ ★ ★ ★

ANSWERS: 1. *d*, 2. *a*, 3. *b*, 4. *b*, 5. *b*, 6. *e*, 7. *b*, 8. *c*, 9. *b*, 10. *c*, 11. *a*, 12. *c*, 13. *c*, 14. *a*, 15. *b*, 16. *a*, 17. *b*, 18. *b*, 19. *a*, 20. *c*, 21. *a*, 22. *c*, 23. *b*, 24. *c*, 25. *b*, 26. *c*, 27. *c*, 28. *e*, 29. *c*, 30. *c*, 31. *c*, 32. *b*, 33. *b*, 34. *c*, 35. *c*.

THE MEANING
OF "IS"

Match the woman with what she said about **BILL CLINTON.**

1. Gennifer Flowers.

a. In 1991, during what she says she thought was going to be a job interview in his hotel room, he dropped his pants, exposed his erect penis—which, she later recalled, had the distinguishing characteristic of being bent—and demanded that she "kiss it."

2. Paula Jones.

b. During a 1993 meeting in a study off of the Oval Office, he kissed her on the mouth, fondled her breast, and put her hand on his penis—all activities that confidante Linda Tripp said she'd been happy about at the time.

3. Juanita Broaddrick.

c. They had a twelve-year affair that ended in 1989.

4. Kathleen Willey.

d. He raped her in 1978 during his first campaign for the governorship of Arkansas, biting her lip in the process and telling her afterward to put some ice on it.

5. Monica Lewinsky.

e. He stuck a cigar in her vagina.

6. What did Gennifer Flowers reveal about Bill Clinton in the interview accompanying her nude spread in *Penthouse*? (Yes, *Penthouse*, because Clinton liked his women to be trashy in a way that *Playboy* didn't like its women to be.)

    a. "We made love everywhere: on the floor, in bed, in the kitchen, on the cabinet and on the sink."

    b. She rated him a "9" as a lover.

    c. Both of the above, plus, "He ate pussy like a champ. I'd have to say, 'Whoa, boy, come on up here.'"

7. What was one of the main things Bill Clinton liked about Gennifer Flowers?

    a. "She was a better singer than her career would have you believe. You know, sometimes those women singing in the Holiday Inns have more talent than you think."

    b. "[She had] an unbelievable sense of humor. I'm telling you, that gal was funny."

    c. "[She] could suck a tennis ball through a garden hose."

8. Who was the *60 Minutes* correspondent who conducted the January 1992 post–Super Bowl interview in which Bill Clinton kind of admitted having had affairs, and Hillary kind of admitted that she knew, without either of them actually officially doing either?

    a. Mike Wallace.

    b. Steve Kroft.

    c. Morley Safer.

9. With Bill Clinton poised to accept the nomination for a second term as president in August 1996, longtime adviser **DICK MORRIS** was the subject of a *Time* cover story, "The Man Who Has Clinton's Ear." In what other publication was an image of him prominently featured that same week, and in what capacity?

 a. The *New York Observer* caricatured him as the Wizard of Oz.

 b. *The Onion* used him as its central figure in a collage of very short men with very big egos.

 c. The tabloid *Star* published photos of him on a Washington, D.C., hotel balcony with a prostitute.

10. According to the *Star*, how did Dick Morris impress his prostitute—yes, *impress his prostitute!*—Sherry Rowlands?

 a. He told her before it was made public that NASA had found evidence that there was life on Mars.

 b. He told her in advance about Clinton's antitobacco offensive.

 c. He let her read an advance draft of Hillary Clinton's convention speech.

 d. All of the above, and as if it all wasn't impressive enough, he let her listen in on his phone calls with President Clinton.

11. What did Sherry Rowlands hear after Dick Morris self-importantly let her listen in on a phone call he placed to President Clinton on the private residential White House line?

 a. Clinton praised Morris and said, "I wouldn't even be up for reelection, let alone be the big favorite, if it wasn't for you."

 b. Clinton went on and on about "this pudgy Jewess who gives me head."

 c. Clinton got on the phone all pissed off and told Morris to use the regular White House lines and not to call the private residence anymore.

12. What did Washington lobbyist Art Roberts say about the Dick Morris/Sherry Rowlands scandal?

  a. "'Sleazy Politician Caught with Hooker.' There's a real dog-bites-man story."

  b. "He was such an insufferable, pompous ass. Everyone in town is high on schadenfreude."

  c. "How can you tell which one was the prostitute?"

13. In addition to revealing his slobbering over her toes, Rowlands told the *Star* that one night Dick Morris got down on all fours and said, _____

  a. "Arf arf."

  b. "This is how masochists propose."

  c. "Can you imagine someone walking in and seeing this?"

14. What distinction does Dick Morris hold?

  a. He's one of the shortest guys ever to star in a tabloid sex scandal.

  b. As far as American political scandals go, he *owns* toe-sucking.

  c. Both of the above, plus he's one of the very few non-presidents (among the others, O. J. Simpson) to be on the cover of *Time* two weeks in a row, the second time under the headline "The Morris Mess: After the Fall," with the wife who would divorce him four months later still standing stoically behind him.

15. What other skeleton tumbled out of Dick Morris's closet as a result of the media scrutiny surrounding the Sherry Rowlands unfortunateness?

    a. He'd fathered an illegitimate daughter—his only child—during a fifteen-year affair with a Texas woman.

    b. He had nipple rings.

    c. He was into autoerotic asphyxiation.

16. Which of these ludicrous predictions was made by Dick Morris?

    a. Hillary Clinton's supporters would "never forgive Obama, especially now that they can vote for Palin."

    b. His marriage could "survive a little toe-sucking."

    c. George W. Bush would "rebound big time" from the Hurricane Katrina fiasco because "every day for the next year, voters will see nonstop scenes of federal relief, rebuilding, renovation and reconstruction along with the empathy, sympathy and compassion these efforts imply in the heart of George W. Bush. . . . Responding to disasters is a source of presidential strength and popularity, and Bush is about to show how it is done." Yeah, *that* happened.

Who's who?

17. Linda Tripp.   **a.** The billionaire newspaper publisher who funded various investigations and reports that led to Bill Clinton's impeachment.

18. Larry Patterson.   **b.** The judge who summarily dismissed Paula Jones's sexual harassment suit against Bill Clinton on the grounds that she was unable to demonstrate that she suffered any damages.

19. Richard Mellon
Scaife.

c. The Arkansas state trooper assigned to Bill Clinton's detail whose job included facilitating tawdry rendezvous with his various girlfriends, such as the time a woman drove up to the governor's mansion in a pickup truck, and Clinton came out and got in the front seat for his blow job, and the trooper watched the whole thing on a TV monitor.

20. Susan Webber
Wright.

d. The Arkansas state trooper who escorted Paula Jones to Bill Clinton's hotel room and waited outside until she came out.

21. Lucianne Goldberg.

e. The betraying friend who wore a wire while Monica Lewinsky idiotically burbled all of the details of her sex with Bill Clinton.

22. Danny Ferguson.

f. The ideologue who urged her friend to betray Monica Lewinsky and wondered, "Do you think there's a taping system in the Oval Office? . . . The slurping sounds would be deafening."

23. How did Monica Lewinsky signal her availability to President Clinton on November 15, 1995?

    a. She left a note on his desk that read, "I WANT U."

    b. She looked at him meaningfully and sucked on her middle finger.

    c. She flashed her thong underwear.

24. Put these events between Monica Lewinsky and President Clinton in chronological order.

   a. She asked him if their relationship was "just about sex, or do you have some interest in trying to get to know me as a person?" He used the word "cherish" to describe his feelings about their time together. They shared a moment of sorrow about the death of the first American soldier in Bosnia. She fellated him not to completion, then accidentally walked in on him later and found him masturbating.

   b. She wanted to see him but was told he was meeting with his lawyers; then she found out that Eleanor Mondale was visiting him in the Oval Office and she had a jealousy fit.

   c. She fellated him while he talked on the phone, but not to "completion" because he didn't trust her enough to come in front of her.

   d. He called her at home and they had their first phone sex.

   e. Use was made of one of the president's cigars.

   f. She finally got her wish and they had a lengthy postcoital conversation, which may well have backfired. As Jeffrey Toobin wrote in *A Vast Conspiracy*, "An actual conversation with Lewinsky may have been the thing that cured the president of his infatuation, because the next time he summoned Lewinsky, two weeks later, it was to break off their relationship," though it continued on and off for months.

   g. She told him she'd been fired from her White House job, and he said if he got reelected he'd bring her back to the White House and she could do "anything you want," and she said, "Well, can I be the assistant to the president for blow jobs?" and he said, "I'd like that." Then she blew him while he talked to Dick Morris, and who knows what was going on at the other end of that call?

h. She was wearing a blue Gap dress and she "finished" him for the first time and . . . well, you know.

Match the number with what it quantifies.

25. 1.   **a.** Sexual encounters Monica Lewinsky says she had with President Clinton, though he says it's one less.

26. 9.   **b.** Days President Clinton's Senate trial ran before he was acquitted of perjury and obstruction of justice charges.

27. 21.   **c.** Days between President Clinton's wagging his finger and saying, "I want to say one thing to the American people. I want you to listen to me. I'm going to say this again: I did not have sexual relations with that woman—Miss Lewinsky" and his telling the grand jury that when he was deposed in the Paula Jones case and his lawyer said, "There is absolutely no sex of any kind" between him and Monica Lewinsky, what he was thinking when he let that statement stand was that whatever relationship there had been was at that point no more—he wasn't saying there never was one, he was saying there isn't one now, which there wasn't—so it was not perjury because "it depends on what the meaning of the word 'is' is."

28. 203.   **d.** Stained dresses saved but not cleaned by Monica Lewinsky.

29. False or true? During one of their postcoital conversations, President Clinton noted that Monica's combat boots were "like Chelsea's."

   a. False. Wouldn't that be a little creepy?
   b. True. He was actually able to conjure up an image of his sixteen-year-old daughter while cheating on her mother with a twenty-two-year-old. Impressive.

30. True or false? Before he wound up obsessing over Bill Clinton's sex life, special prosecutor Kenneth Starr had been involved in the O. J. Simpson case.

   a. True. He consulted with regard to the DNA evidence.
   b. False. Before he wound up obsessing over Bill Clinton's sex life, he'd been called in by the Senate ethics committee to work on the investigation into Bob Packwood's sexual misconduct, and it fell to him to read Packwood's diaries. An objective observer could certainly conclude that Kenneth Starr is unnaturally attracted to the skeevy.

★ ★ ★ ★ ★

ANSWERS: 1. *c*, 2. *a*, 3. *d*, 4. *b*, 5. *e*, 6. *c*, 7. *c*, 8. *b*, 9. *c*, 10. *d*, 11. *c*, 12. *c*, 13. *c*, 14. *c*, 15. *a*, 16. *c*, 17. *e*, 18. *c*, 19. *a*, 20. *b*, 21. *f*, 22. *d*, 23. *c*, 24. *c, d, a, f, e, g, h, b*, 25. *d*, 26. *a*, 27. *b*, 28. *c*, 29. *b*, 30. *b*.

THE CADS

239

1. True or false? After five and a half years of imprisonment, ex-POW **JOHN MCCAIN**'s 1973 homecoming to his wife and three kids was a completely joyous event.

   a. True. Pure bliss.

   b. False. While he was obviously delighted to be back in America, there was an unhappy surprise waiting for him. His beautiful swimwear model wife, Carol, had been in a disfiguring car accident four years earlier, and when he got off the plane there was his formerly tall and beautiful model wife on crutches, four inches shorter, and considerably heavier.

2. How did John McCain react to the misfortunes of the wife who had undergone almost unspeakable physical hardship while also raising their children in his absence?

   a. He swore undying loyalty to her.

   b. He dedicated his career to helping the handicapped.

   c. He had lots of affairs and then in 1979 he began an affair with Cindy Lou Hensley, the beer heiress he would go on to marry whose family's money would finance his political career, and whose teasing about his thinning hair he would one day react to very badly by snarling at her in front of strangers, "At least I don't plaster on the makeup like a trollop, you cunt."

3. Four of these statements about John McCain were made by Ted Sampley, a veteran of the U.S. Special Forces in Vietnam. Which one was uttered by Ross Perot, who paid Carol's medical bills while McCain was held captive?

   a. "I have been following John McCain's career for nearly twenty years. I know him personally. There is something wrong with this guy and let me tell you what it is—deceit."

b. "When he came home and saw that Carol was not the beauty he left behind, he started running around on her almost right away. Everybody around him knew it."

c. "Eventually he met Cindy and she was young and beautiful and very wealthy. At that point McCain just dumped Carol for something he thought was better."

d. "This is a guy who makes such a big deal about his character. He has no character. He is a fake. If there was any character in that first marriage, it all belonged to Carol."

e. "McCain is the classic opportunist. He's always reaching for attention and glory. After he came home, Carol walked with a limp. So he threw her over for a poster girl with big money from Arizona. And the rest is history."

4. False or true? In 1998 John McCain told a really hideous joke at the expense of then-seventeen-year-old Chelsea Clinton that was wildly indicative of his true feelings about women.

a. False. McCain was far too invested in his own image as a man of honor to stoop so low.

b. True. "Do you know why Chelsea Clinton is so ugly? Because Janet Reno is her father."

5. False or true? The 2008 *New York Times* story implying that John McCain had an affair with lobbyist Vicki Iseman was actually a good thing for him.

a. False. It just served to remind people about what a pig he'd been with his first wife.

b. True. All the attention was focused on the not-all-that-convincing sexual accusation, and the really damaging part of the story—the favors he did for the pretty lobbyist whose clients had business before the committee he chaired—went basically unexamined.

6. False or true? Vicki Iseman sued the *New York Times* for $27 million over that article.

    a. False. She assumed people forgot about stuff like that right away.

    b. True. Apparently it was that important to her that not even a single person who might have seen the article think of her as someone who would let John McCain have sex with her. Ultimately, no money changed hands.

Who's who in the life of New York mayor **RUDY GIULIANI?**

7. Regina Peruggi.

    a. His first wife, to whom he was married for fourteen years before finding out that she was not, as he said he'd believed, his third cousin, but rather his second cousin—a confusion that occurred, he explained, "because I never calculated the lines of consanguinity . . . I don't think we ever discussed it in any great detail," and which realization came, oddly enough, in the midst of his committing adultery with the woman who would soon become his second wife.

8. Howard Koeppel.

    b. His second wife, who learned of his intention to end their marriage along with the rest of the world's population when he announced it at a press conference.

9. Donna Hanover.

c. His communications director, with whom he was widely believed to have been cheating on his second wife before cheating on his second wife with the woman who would become his third wife.

10. Judith Nathan.

d. Half of the gay couple he moved in with when his second wife refused to move out of Gracie Mansion following his graceless announcement that he wanted out of the marriage.

11. Cristyne Lategano.

e. His third wife, whose adulterous relationship with him before their marriage entitled her to chauffeur service from the New York City Police Department.

12. True or false? During his wooing of Judith Nathan, Rudy Giuliani was scrupulously careful to keep his personal and professional expenses separate.

   a. True. It was part of what made him such a super mayor.

   b. False. He billed various obscure city agencies for the tens of thousands of dollars in security expenses incurred by his weekend visits to her Southampton spread.

13. Unaware in May 2001 that four months later the single worst event in American history would make Rudy Giuliani a national hero ("America's mayor!"), what did his attorney do in an effort to minimize the impact of the PR disaster that was the ghastly public ending of his second marriage?

a. He revealed, with Giuliani's permission, that the treatments he'd been undergoing for prostate cancer had rendered him impotent for the past year, so he hadn't had sex with Ms. Nathan in a year.

b. He convinced Giuliani to work four hours a week in a women's shelter.

c. He got several editors to run stories about Giuliani's fondness for performing in drag, believing that this little quirk humanized him.

14. How did Rudy Giuliani's police commissioner **BERNARD KERIK** distinguish himself during his sixteen-month tenure?

a. He oversaw the police response to the 9/11 attacks.

b. He oversaw a huge drop in violent crime in New York City.

c. Both of the above, though he's most famous for using an apartment donated for the use of 9/11 rescue workers as a trysting place for his affair with publisher Judith Regan.

Who said what about Rudy Giuliani?

15. Schools Chancellor (and former Giuliani pal) Rudy Crew.

a. "It's like his goal in life is to spear people, destroy them, to go for the jugular."

16. *Newsday* columnist Jimmy Breslin.

b. "It's like a cult he's got there. You can't work with the guy unless you're willing to drink the Kool-Aid."

17. Former New York City police commissioner William Bratton.

c. "There's obviously a little problem that exists between me and his [third] wife."

18. His twenty-one-year-old son Andrew.

d. "This is a maniac. . . . He is not bound by the truth. I have studied animal life, and their predator/prey relations are more graceful than his."

19. Former mayor Ed Koch, author of *Giuliani: Nasty Man.*

e. "[He] didn't bring us together, our pain brought us together and our decency brought us together. We would have come together if Bozo was the mayor."

20. Professional black man Al Sharpton.

f. "A small man in search of a balcony."

21. *Los Angeles* magazine columnist John Powers.

g. "[His] Nixonian soul comes bearing the face of a particularly cruel Renaissance cardinal."

22. False or true? **NEWT GINGRICH** won his congressional seat in 1978 by running a family-values campaign in which he said his opponent would leave her family behind in Georgia if elected, while *he* would keep *his* family together.

 a. False. He was far too aware of the pitfalls of public life to make such a promise.

 b. True, which was ironic, of course, because it was well known that he was sleeping around and his marriage was doomed.

23. Newt Gingrich had a crush on his high school math teacher, Jackie Battley, who was seven years older than he. He married her in 1962, when he was nineteen, and let her work to put him through school while also raising their two daughters. At some point he realized that, as he told a friend, "she isn't young or pretty enough to be the President's wife," and he walked out on her in 1980, thereby breaking his first campaign promise. How did she find out that her marriage was over?

   a. Gingrich took her to a fancy restaurant, ordered a bottle of Dom Perignon, asked if she wanted to renew their marriage vows, and when she said yes, responded, "Well, I don't! It's over!"

   b. Gingrich deliberately left a receipt from an extramarital hotel tryst for her to find.

   c. Gingrich showed up at her hospital bedside (where she was recovering from her third surgery for uterine cancer) with a yellow legal pad on which he'd written down the details of the divorce that would allow him to marry one of the women with whom he'd been committing adultery.

Sort out Newt Gingrich's women.

24. Marianne Ginther. **a.** The married volunteer who got involved with him during his second campaign, and who told *Vanity Fair's* Gail Sheehy—who wrote the definitive Gingrich profile in 1995—that he preferred oral sex "because then he can say, 'I never slept with her.'"

25. Anne Manning. **b.** The member of his staff who in 1981 became, for almost twenty years, his second wife, and who said, "I don't want him to be president and I don't think he should be."

26. False or true? After they had oral sex, Newt Gingrich warned Anne Manning, "If you ever tell anybody about this, I'll say you're lying."

    a. False. You don't threaten someone who's just given you a blow job.

    b. True. "He's morally dishonest," she said of him. "He has gone too far believing that 'I'm beyond the law.' He should be stopped before it's too late."

27. What amusing anecdote did Newt Gingrich's campaign treasurer Kip Carter recount to Gail Sheehy?

    a. He recalled one time when Newt "almost got the shit kicked out of him at a bar—you can see where he's the kind of guy that could happen to, and when he's drunk you can multiply that by a thousand."

    b. He recalled one time when Newt had stopped at a Denny's before giving a really important speech and "he spilled a bowl of pea soup all over himself, and he didn't have a change of clothes and mine didn't fit him, so he had to give his talk wearing this sopping wet green-stained shirt."

    c. He recalled one time in the 1970s after a local Friday night high school football game, when "I had Newt's daughters, Jackie Sue and Kathy, with me. We were all supposed to meet back at this professor's house. . . . I was cutting across the yard to go up the driveway. There was a car there. As I got to the car, I saw Newt in the passenger seat and one of the guys' wives with her head in his lap going up and down. Newt kind of turned and gave me his little-boy smile. Fortunately [his daughters] were a lot younger and shorter then."

28. How did Marianne Gingrich find out that her marriage was over?

   a. She turned on the TV and saw Newt announcing it at a press conference.

   b. She received an e-mail from Newt with the subject line, "Divorce."

   c. She was in Ohio celebrating her mother's eighty-fourth birthday. The phone rang. Her mother answered. Newt Gingrich wished her a happy birthday, then asked to talk to his wife, who had recently been diagnosed with multiple sclerosis. She got on the phone. He told her he wanted a divorce.

29. In 2000 Newt Gingrich married twenty-three-years-his-junior congressional aide Callista Bisek, with whom he'd not only been committing adultery, but with whom he'd been committing adultery the whole time he was in high dudgeon about President Clinton's immorality with Monica Lewinsky. What thought must occur to Callista Gingrich at least once in a while?

   a. "Newt is such a gentleman."

   b. "I'm the luckiest woman alive."

   c. "I better not get sick."

*Even as John Kerry's 2004 running mate, **JOHN EDWARDS**, was in the midst of his own presidential race, this blind item appeared in the* New York Post's *"Page Six": "Which political candidate enjoys visiting New York because he has a girlfriend who lives downtown? The pol tells her he'll marry her when his current wife is out of the picture." For a year, the story of Edwards's affair was known by everyone in the blogosphere even as the mainstream press fastidiously avoided it. Then . . .*

30. What happened after John Edwards met the new-agey-yet-trashy party girl Rielle Hunter in a New York bar in late 2005?

  a. They very quickly had sex.

  b. He hired her to follow him around with a video camera and edit his wisdom down into campaign "webisodes," and just generally be around all the time for lots of sex.

  c. Hunter told pretty much anyone who would listen that she was in love with John Edwards.

  d. Hunter told a *Newsweek* reporter that John Edwards's wife, Elizabeth, "does not give off good energy" and that "someday the truth about her is going to come out."

  e. Someone on the campaign walked in on Edwards and Hunter in a compromising enough position that word got back to Elizabeth Edwards.

  f. Edwards claims that he confessed the affair to Elizabeth unbidden, though a far likelier scenario is that she read him the riot act.

  g. Edwards claims that nothing more happened, though evidence indicates that in fact the affair resumed even as he was beginning his presidential race.

  h. Hunter told the *Newsweek* reporter that she was working on a "genius" TV show idea about "women who help men get out of failing marriages by having affairs with them."

i. Edwards dismissed a *National Enquirer* story about the affair as "made up" and said of Elizabeth, "I've been in love with the same woman for 30-plus years, and as anybody who's been around us knows, she's an extraordinary human being, warm, loving, beautiful, sexy and as good a person as I have ever known. So the story's just false."

j. Hunter had a baby girl. The father's name was not listed on the birth certificate.

k. A former Edwards campaign aide claimed paternity of the child.

l. Hunter began receiving $15,000 a month from the former finance chairman of the failed 2008 presidential campaign.

m. The *Enquirer*, having received word that Edwards would be visiting Hunter and her mysteriously fathered daughter at a Beverly Hills hotel, sent reporters who confirmed that Edwards was indeed there, and when he tried to leave at 2:40 A.M. via the basement, as they reported, "he was greeted by several reporters. . . . Without saying anything, Edwards ran up the stairs leading from the hotel basement to the lobby. But, spotting a photographer, he doubled back into the basement. As he emerged from the stairwell, reporter Butterfield questioned him about his hookup with Rielle. Edwards did not answer and then ran into a nearby restroom. He stayed inside for about 15 minutes, refusing to answer questions . . . about what he was doing in the hotel. A group of hotel security men eventually escorted him from the men's room, while preventing . . . reporters from following him out of the hotel."

n. In the hope that the story would get less coverage, John Edwards issued his statement admitting the affair on the day that the Beijing Olympics started.

o. Edwards said in his statement that "Being 99 percent honest is no longer enough," though it was hard to see where he got that figure from, given that he'd actually been o percent honest before then and was still lying about the length and intensity of the affair, not to mention the whole paternity thing.

p. Edwards went on *Nightline* and dismissed an *Enquirer* photo seeming to show him holding the baby widely believed to be his love child by asking, "Do you know how many pictures have been taken of me holding children in the last three years? I mean, it happens all the time," as if this late-night hotel room rendezvous with a mistress were merely another campaign event.

q. All of the above, plus Edwards said he'd be "happy" to take a paternity test, but wouldn't you know it, Hunter said she wouldn't allow it.

31. In which Beverly Hills hotel did the Edwards/Hunter rendezvous take place?
   a. The Beverly Hills.
   b. The Beverly Wilshire.
   c. The Beverly Hilton.

Who's who?

32. Gary Pearce.

a. The campaign aide who fell on his sword, as it were, for John Edwards.

33. Fred Baron.

b. The payer of the $15,000 monthly non-child-support payments.

34. Pidgeon O'Brien.

c. The friend of Rielle Hunter who told CBS News that the affair had gone on much longer and was much more serious than John Edwards's statement implied.

35. David Carr.

d. The sister of Rielle Hunter who said the baby "looks like John Edwards. She's got his eyes and jaw line and lips."

36. Andrew Young.

e. The *New York Times* reporter who lauded the *Enquirer* for exposing a story that the mainstream media were too squeamish to go after, saying, "It would be hard to argue that the body politic is not enriched by the recent revelations that Mr. Edwards is not who we thought he was," and pointing out that "even in his confession, Mr. Edwards wrinkled his nose and suggested that the allegations had originated with 'supermarket tabloids,' as if the method of conveyance absolved him of the deeds described."

37. Roxanne Druck Marshall.

f. The manager of John Edwards's 1998 Senate campaign, who said, "If it's not true, he's got to stand up and say, 'This is not true. That is not my child and I'm going to take legal action against the people who are spreading these lies.' It's not enough to say, 'That's tabloid trash.'"

38. How did Rielle Hunter refer to John Edwards in e-mails to friends boasting of her affair?

   a. "Boy Toy."

   b. "Love Lips."

   c. "My Baby Dada."

39. True or false? At one point during the *Nightline* interview, John Edwards reached for the hand of his wife, Elizabeth, and she pulled it away.

   a. True. It was an exhilarating moment—some viewers reported that they stood up and cheered.

   b. False. She knew better than to be anywhere near the camera; he took that bullet alone.

40. What happened during the *Nightline* interview?

   a. John Edwards repeatedly asked Bob Woodruff, "Can I explain what happened?" when of course it was the very reason he was there.

   b. John Edwards admitted sleeping with Rielle Hunter but denied loving her, apparently thinking this lack of gallantry somehow mitigated his betrayal of his wife.

   c. John Edwards actually pointed out that Elizabeth Edwards's cancer was in remission at the time of the affair, so, you know, it's not like he was cheating on a dying woman.

   d. John Edwards declared that "none of" the members of his family was responsible for his cheating, lest anyone think that maybe somehow his young children had caused it.

   e. All of the above, plus John Edwards reminded people that John McCain had cheated on his first wife, though he didn't mention McCain publicly calling his second wife a "cunt."

41. True or false? During the Clinton impeachment hearings, John Edwards defended the president, calling the proceedings a "witch hunt."

   a. True. His first speech from the Senate floor was a defense of Clinton.

   b. False. Edwards piously intoned, "I think this president has shown a remarkable disrespect for his office, for the moral dimensions of leadership, for his friends, for his wife, for his precious daughter. It is breathtaking to me the level to which that disrespect has risen."

42. True or false? When North Carolina senator John Edwards was angling to become John Kerry's running mate in 2004, he told him a story about his son Wade—who'd been killed in a car accident eight years earlier—that moved Kerry to tears.

   a. True. Kerry had been leaning toward picking Richard Gephardt, but he decided on the spot to switch to Edwards.

   b. False. Edwards prefaced the heartrending story—about climbing onto the medical examiner's table, lying next to his son's body, hugging him, and promising that he'd devote himself to improving people's lives as Wade would have done—by telling Kerry he was going to tell him something he'd never told a living soul, so Kerry was seriously creeped out when he realized that Edwards had, a year or two earlier, related the exact same story almost verbatim. Then, with the shrewd judgment that told him the most effective way to deal with the Swift Boat attacks on his character was to ignore them, he put Edwards on the ticket anyway.

43. Imagine that you maxed out your donation to the 2008 John Edwards campaign. How do you suppose you would have felt upon learning that the guy you believed in—the guy you thought was qualified to be president—turned out to be so unutterably stupid that he thought he could keep his cheating on his cancer-ridden wife a secret from the voracious gossip industry and the stop-at-nothing psychos he'd have been running against?

 a. Whew! Did we dodge a bullet there, or what? If this dick had won the nomination, he would have just handed the election to John McCain.
 b. Completely duped. How could I not have seen it before? He's so smarmy he spreads smarmalade on his toast.
 c. Furious. I want my fucking money back.
 d. All of the above, don't you think?

44. Which of these spectacularly un-self-aware statements by the candidate from the campaign films made by John Edwards's mistress was the first thing to be heard in the first film?

 a. "I'd rather be successful or unsuccessful based on who I really am, not based on some plastic Ken doll that you put up in front of audiences. That's not me, you know?"
 b. "I want to see our party lead on the great moral is-sues—yes, me, a Democrat, using that word—the great moral issues that face our country."
 c. "This"—this being following him around all the time recording his every inane bleat for posterity—"I abso-lutely believe has the potential of changing the way people do this"—this being campaign for president—"in a very good way. A very good way."
 d. "I've come to the personal conclusion that I actually want the country to see who I am, who I really am. But I don't know what the result of that will be."

45. True or false? The theme song for John Edwards's webisode series was "Born in the U.S.A."

a. True. There was some hope of parlaying it into a Springsteen endorsement, but that didn't eventuate.

b. False. The song was "True Reflections," with the in-retrospect-brutal lyrics, "When you look into a mirror/ do you like what's lookin' at you?/Now that you've seen your true reflection/what on earth are you gonna do?" Oh, my.

★ ★ ★ ★ ★

ANSWERS: 1. *b*, 2. *c*, 3. *e*, 4. *b*, 5. *b*, 6. *b*, 7. *a*, 8. *d*, 9. *b*, 10. *e*, 11. *c*, 12. *b*, 13. *a*, 14. *c*, 15. *d*, 16. *f*, 17. *b*, 18. *c*, 19. *a*, 20. *e*, 21. *g*, 22. *b*, 23. *c*, 24. *b*, 25. *a*, 26. *b*, 27. *c*, 28. *c*, 29. *c*, 30. *q*, 31. *c*, 32. *f*, 33. *b*, 34. *c*, 35. *e*, 36. *a*, 37. *d*, 38. *b*, 39. *b*, 40. *e*, 41. *b*, 42. *b*, 43. *d*, 44. *d*, 45. *b*.

ACKNOWLEDGMENTS

Thanks to David Rosenthal for his instant enthusiasm, David McCormick for taking care of business, and Colin Fox for his severely tested patience. And thanks to Google, Nexis, and Wikipedia, without any of which this would have been a much tougher slog.

STRANGE BEDFELLOWS

STRANGE BEDFELLOWS

ABOUT THE AUTHOR

PAUL SLANSKY, a frequent contributor to *The New Yorker*, is the author of several books, including *The Clothes Have No Emperor,* a *New York Times* bestseller about the Reagan presidency, and *The George W. Bush Quiz Book.* His work has appeared in dozens of publications, including the *New York Observer, Spy, Esquire, Newsweek, Playboy, The New York Times, Rolling Stone,* and *The New Republic,* and on The Huffington Post and Time .com. He lives in Los Angeles with his wife, Liz Dubelman, and their daughter, Grace.

Printed in the United States
By Bookmasters